COMPETITION POLICY AND THE DEREGULATION OF ROAD TRANSPORT

ORGANISATION FOR ECONOMIC CO-OPERATION AND DEVELOPMENT

Pursuant to article 1 of the Convention signed in Paris on 14th December 1960, and which came into force on 30th September 1961, the Organisation for Economic Co-operation and Development (OECD) shall promote policies designed:

- to achieve the highest sustainable economic growth and employment and a rising standard of living in Member countries, while maintaining financial stability, and thus to contribute to the development of the world economy;
- to contribute to sound economic expansion in Member as well as non-member countries in the process of economic development; and
- to contribute to the expansion of world trade on a multilateral, non-discriminatory basis in accordance with international obligations.

The original Member countries of the OECD are Austria, Belgium, Canada, Denmark, France, the Federal Republic of Germany, Greece, Iceland, Ireland, Italy, Luxembourg, the Netherlands, Norway, Portugal, Spain, Sweden, Switzerland, Turkey, the United Kingdom and the United States. The following countries became Members subsequently through accession at the dates indicated hereafter: Japan (28th April 1964), Finland (28th January 1969), Australia (7th June 1971) and New Zealand (29th May 1973).

The Socialist Federal Republic of Yugoslavia takes part in some of the work of the OECD (agreement of 28th October 1961).

Publié en français sous le titre:

POLITIQUE DE LA CONCURRENCE
ET DÉRÉGLEMENTATION
DES TRANSPORTS ROUTIERS

This report by the Committee on Competition Law and Policy examines the impact of regulatory reform of both the freight and passenger segments of the road transport industry in OECD countries and the implications of these reforms for competition policy. It is based essentially on replies to a questionnaire received from 19 countries - Australia, Belgium, Canada, Denmark, Finland, France, Germany, Greece, Ireland, Italy, Japan, New Zealand, Norway, Portugal, Spain, Sweden, Switzerland, United Kingdom and the United States - and from the Commission of the European Communities as well as on economic literature on the effects of deregulation in various countries. The report generally reflects the situation as of 31st December 1989.

The OECD Council agreed to the derestriction of this report on 27th July 1990.

Also available

COMPETITION POLICY IN OECD COUNTRIES — 1987/1988 (1989)
(24 89 01 1) ISBN 92–64–13192–2   FF160   £19.50   US$34.00   DM66

COMPETITION POLICY AND INTELLECTUAL PROPERTY RIGHTS (1989)
(24 89 03 1) ISBN 92–64–13242–2   FF90   £11.00   US$19.00   DM37

PREDATORY PRICING (1989)
(24 89 02 1) ISBN 92–64–13245–7   FF70   £8.50   US$15.00   DM29

DEREGULATION AND AIRLINE COMPETITION (1988)
(24 88 02 1) ISBN 92–64–13101–9   FF100   £12.00   US$22.00   DM43

INTERNATIONAL MERGERS AND COMPETITION POLICY (1988)
(24 88 03 3) ISBN 92–64–03143–X   FF90   £11.00   US$20.00   DM39

THE COSTS OF RESTRICTING IMPORTS: The Automobile Industry (1988)
(24 87 06 1) ISBN 92–64–13037–3   FF85   £8.50   US$18.00   DM36

COMPETITION POLICY AND JOINT VENTURES (1987)
(24 86 03 1) ISBN 92–64–12898–0   FF65   £6.50   US$13.00   DM29

Forthcoming

COMPETITION POLICY IN OECD COUNTRIES — 1988/1989

Prices charged at the OECD Bookshop.

*The OECD CATALOGUE OF PUBLICATIONS and supplements will be sent free of charge
on request addressed either to OECD Publications Service,
2, rue André–Pascal, 75775 PARIS CEDEX 16, or to the OECD Distributor in your country.*

COMPETITION POLICY AND THE DEREGULATION OF ROAD TRANSPORT

TABLE OF CONTENTS

CHAPTER 4 - HOW COMPETITION LAWS AND POLICIES APPLY TO ROAD TRANSPORT

SUMMARY AND CONCLUSIONS

SUMMARY

1.   This report is concerned with the economic regulation of the road transport industry, both freight and passenger transport. By economic regulation is meant regulation of who may operate in the industry, the services or routes that are to be provided and the charges that may be made. In many OECD countries economic regulation has been reduced in recent years, if not removed altogether, with the aim of encouraging competition and efficiency. Such developments need not have adverse consequences for safety or the environment which may be protected more efficiently by direct controls not involving economic regulation.

2.   Road transport is an important sector of all OECD countries. The growth of road freight transport in the 1970s and 1980s has been spectacular, scarcely interrupted by the oil shocks of 1973 and 1979 or by the recession in the early 1980s. This growth has been largely at the expense of railways and can be explained by the greater flexibility of road transport in providing a wide range of services for different types of services and a broader geographical coverage. Improved road networks and larger and more efficient vehicles have contributed to the cost advantage of road over rail for all but the longer journeys. In contrast to freight, passenger road transport seems in many countries to be an industry in long-term decline, mainly as a result of the growth of private car ownership. On some routes, passenger services also face competition from railways or airlines.

3.   An analysis of regulation requires consideration of the structure of the regulated industry. In all OECD countries road freight transport has the structural characteristics of a competitive industry. Economies of scale or scope are not significant, relative to most industries, and costs of entry to the industry are minimal. Despite such developments as hub and spoke patterns of operation in long haul freight transport, the industry is generally unconcentrated and has remained so in most sectors in those countries where the industry has been largely deregulated. Exceptions in some countries are the freight forwarding sector and some specialised transport sectors, which are more concentrated.

4.   On the passenger side there are also few sources of significant economies of scale or scope and the costs of entry are generally low. Ownership or control of strategically sited bus stations could constitute an entry barrier in some instances, as might the brand image and network of services of an established operator. But with such possible exceptions, easy entry suggests that if passenger transport were deregulated (or the operators privatised) a competitive structure could emerge. For local bus services, however, many routes or services provide too little revenue to support several competing operators. The present situation is that many unprofitable local bus

services are sustained only by cross-subsidisation by the operator from other more profitable routes or services or by a general subsidy from the local authority (which often owns or manages the operator in its area) or from central government funds.

5.   Despite the basically competitive nature of both freight and passenger transport, both sectors have until recently been subject to a wide degree of regulation covering the conditions of entry and exit, prices and routes to be operated. The main reason for regulation appears originally, in the 1930s, to have been the fear of the railways that there would be unfair competition from a new and expanding road haulage industry which could not be matched by a regulated railway industry. Hauliers themselves considered that an unregulated haulage industry would lead to "destructive" competition which would force firms into bankruptcy and result in drivers and vehicles being dangerously overdriven.

6.   As regards passenger transport, the main reason for regulation or public ownership has been the public service nature of the industry and the need to provide a network of services to the local community, service to particular destinations or service at particular hours. Safety considerations have also been a reason for regulation of passenger transport.

7.   Regulatory reform of freight transport dates from the 1950s and 1960s in some countries, when the objectives of economic regulation came to be questioned by evidence that it raised the price of transport and thus the price of goods and that it did not demonstrably contribute to greater road safety. During the 1980s several other countries have proceeded to deregulate road haulage, though the extent of reform varies from country to country. However, entry, rate and capacity restrictions still exist in many OECD countries in road haulage.

8.   The passenger transport sector still remains highly regulated in most OECD countries. This is particularly true of local bus services. Only the United Kingdom, since 1985, has proceeded to complete deregulation of local buses, after deregulating long-distance coach services in 1980. As from January and July 1989, some deregulatory steps concerning local and intercity services have been taken in Sweden.

9.   International road haulage and passenger transport in Europe are also generally subject to regulation under bilateral or multilateral agreements between countries which significantly impair international competition. These agreements fix rates and determine quotas for road haulage between the countries concerned by means of a licensing system. There has been some liberalisation within the EEC with quotas being progressively increased under successive regulations and they will be abolished altogether by 1st January 1993. The present cabotage policy of allowing hauliers to pick up and deliver goods in foreign countries, particularly on backhaul trips, on a restricted basis, will be liberalised as from 1st July 1990, while as from 1st January 1990, complete pricing freedom for the transport of goods within the EEC has been introduced. International scheduled road passenger transport is subject to regulation under bilateral agreements while occasional or shuttle services have been partially liberalised. Proposals have also been put forward to allow authorised carriers to provide passenger services in foreign countries.

10.   Road transport services between Canada and the United States are not
restricted by bilateral agreement. Moreover, with respect to freight
transport, a consultative mechanism exists to ensure that neither government
engages in unfair, discriminatory or restrictive practices towards the other's
carriers.

11.   The evidence of the countries which have deregulated their road
transport industries suggests that the benefits are likely to outweigh any
disadvantages, certainly as far as freight is concerned. Causal relationships
are difficult to establish because of concurrent technological and economic
developments, but the observed developments where deregulation has occurred are
consistent with the view that economic regulation has tended to increase costs
and therefore charges. Further, comparisons between regulated and deregulated
performance over the same time periods, for example in the United States as
regards trucking in deregulated states as opposed to regulated ones, or in
Australia and the United Kingdom in relation to "trial" areas of deregulation
of bus services, would seem to point to a significantly better performance in
the deregulated areas.

12.   The deregulation of road freight has been beneficial for both shippers
and consumers and has increased the efficiency of the carriers themselves.
Freight rates have generally declined in real terms following deregulation no
doubt due to an increase in the number of new entrants into the industry
bringing greater competition.   The range of services offered has generally
increased.

13.   There is evidence that the search for efficiency has resulted in a
reduction in real wages to drivers and reduced profits, but employment seems to
benefit.   In the United States, drivers' wages were above the average
industrial wage before deregulation but have since tended towards the average.
This suggests that drivers were sharing the rents created by entry restriction
under regulation. Employment in the industry has generally increased or has
declined less than the average for manufacturing industry in periods of
recession.

14.   Concerns that deregulation of freight transport would lead to
instability in the industry and to "destructive" competition have proved
unfounded.   In the United Kingdom and Sweden, for example, the data suggest
that the rate of turnover of operators has remained remarkably stable since
deregulation.

15.   As to safety, there are many factors at work in addition to any
deregulation.   In view of the growth of traffic, the safety record of the
industry seems good. There is no evidence to suggest that removal of controls
on entry, liberalising of charges and so forth have had any adverse effects
upon safety; nor should this be expected since strict regulation of safety
aspects can be and has been maintained apart from economic deregulation.

16.   The effects of deregulation of long-distance coach services and local
buses are more difficult to assess and there is less experience with
deregulation here than in the freight sector.   In the United States, an
evaluation of the consequences of deregulation must take into consideration the
widespread use of private automobiles and competition from the now deregulated
airline industry. Thus, the US has seen first an increase in the number of new

companies entering the market and then a rapid restructuring of the industry (including, in 1988, the merger of the two largest long-distance carriers) in response to economic conditions. Long-distance coach fares generally fell in the US following deregulation but some services were cut, particularly those serving small communities, continuing a trend that had already begun before deregulation.

17.   In the UK the deregulation of long-distance services in 1980 led to a considerable expansion of the sector: between 1980 and 1985 the number of passengers carried increased from 9 million to 15 million as almost 700 new express coach services were established in the first three years after deregulation. There was a particularly marked expansion in commuter coach services in the greater London area and in some other urban areas in the early years of deregulation. Initially, the growth of the sector was largely at the expense of the railways and deregulation has stimulated more active competition, including price competition, between the two modes of transport. New entry has largely been on a localised basis. The major national carrier did face competition for a period after deregulation on much of its network of routes from a consortium of bus operators. This triggered deep price cuts by the incumbent carrier. The entrant's subsequent withdrawal from the market and the sharp increase in the fares charged by the dominant carrier suggest that scarce terminal facilities in the centre of large cities like London can operate as a significant entry barrier.

18.   Detailed information on the impact of deregulation on local bus services is only available from the United Kingdom and that for a relatively short period since complete deregulation outside London and Northern Ireland took effect only in October 1986. Levels of services have increased in many towns and more vehicle miles have been operated without subsidy, thanks largely to the increased use of competitive tendering for unprofitable services. Reductions in subsidies have led to some increase in fares; on non-subsidized services, fares have generally risen in line with inflation though deregulation has led to fare reductions where new entry has taken place. There has been an increased use of minibuses and a growth in commuter services following deregulation.

19.   The application of competition laws in the past to the road transport sector has been inhibited by the existence of regulatory schemes which approved behaviour that would otherwise have been considered anti-competitive. Road transport therefore enjoyed explicit or implicit exemption from most competition laws. This exemption still continues in many countries but its scope has been increasingly narrowed down by actions to determine the bounds of regulatory policy and competition policy. Thus there has been a certain amount of enforcement particularly against rate or fare-fixing agreements, collusive tendering, practices by dominant firms and, to some extent, mergers, though in the case of mergers, the unconcentrated nature of most sectors of the industry has not yet given rise to prohibition of any acquisition or merger in either the freight or passenger segments. Deregulation of local bus services in the United Kingdom has given rise to several allegations by new entrants of predatory behaviour by incumbent operators. There might be a similar experience if other countries deregulated this sector of the transport industry. As noted in the Committee's recent report, predatory pricing is difficult to distinguish from legitimate competitive behaviour, and a detailed

assessment embracing the structure of the market and the feasibility of a successful strategy of predation, as well as cost-price relationships should be conducted into each case.

CONCLUSIONS AND RECOMMENDATIONS

Road freight

20.   This report shows that there is no remaining rationale for the economic regulation of road freight transport.

21.   *The Committee recommends* that restrictions on entry into freight transport markets should be lifted and that regulation of routes and rates should also be abandoned.

22.   This recommendation does not mean that all forms of regulation of the road freight transport industry should be eliminated. The Committee recognises that there will continue to be a need for regulation aimed to promote safety and to deal with environmental concerns e.g. regulation of driver qualifications and working hours, the condition of vehicles, vehicle weights and loads etc., and regulations relating to noise standards or vehicle emissions. The Committee sees no need for regulation for these purposes to be part of a system of economic regulation of road freight transport; indeed regulation of entry and rates is unlikely to be an efficient way of achieving policy objectives on safety and the environment.

23.   *The Committee also recommends* that any remaining exemptions from competition laws of road freight transport should be removed, and that competition law and policy enforcement should operate in this, as in any other, part of the private sector of the economy.

Road passengers: inter-city services

24.   There also seems no convincing case for regulation of entry, routes and fares of inter-city, long distance bus services. As with freight, there will also be a continuing need for regulation for safety and environmental reasons; but, as with freight, this should be separate from any form of economic regulation.

25.   The report identifies some particular problems that may be encountered by competition authorities when this sector is opened to competition and new entry. An example is the advantage to an established, dominant operator if he has exclusive use of scarce central terminals or bus stations. However, these problems are not unique to the transport sector and can be dealt with in whatever way is appropriate under a country's competition laws.

26.   *The Committee therefore recommends* the deregulation of inter-city bus services, and the removal of any exemption for this sector of the transport industry from competition laws. The Committee recognises however that this Recommendation has implications for other modes of transport, especially for rail transport.

Road passengers: local bus services

27.   There is so far little experience within OECD countries of deregulation of local bus services. Regulation, often coupled with public ownership of a monopoly supplier, is widely seen as the means for ensuring that adequate services are provided to the local community at reasonable levels of fares.

28.   One mechanism for this is internal cross-subsidisation - the more heavily trafficked and profitable services providing the revenue to support uneconomic services. The Committee recognises the social policy objectives which lead to cross-subsidisation. But cross-subsidisation is an inefficient way of providing uneconomic services for which there is considered to be a social need. And the true costs of this method of provision are concealed. In principle specific subsidies can be given by the municipal or other public authority to those operators willing to provide uneconomic services, and in principle these subsidies can be offered to competitive tender, the contract being awarded to whichever operator is willing to provide the specified level of service for the lowest level of subsidy. This is the approach taken in the United Kingdom with some success since 1986.

29.   The Committee recognises the social and urban development concerns that may lead the public authorities to ensure the provision of a network of services. Nevertheless regulation has its costs. Taking into account recent experience (mainly in the United Kingdom), *the Committee recommends* that existing regulatory arrangements and exemptions of local bus services from competition laws should be critically reviewed and the case for deregulation given serious consideration.

30.   The United Kingdom experience suggests that it will take time for an industry which has for so long been subject to detailed economic regulation, and often to close political control, to adjust to the opportunities and challenges offered by deregulation. Competition authorities are likely to be faced, for example, with allegations of predatory behaviour or other abuses of a dominant position by established operators, and with pressures to condone cooperative arrangements between erstwhile competing operators, for example to agree fares on competing as well as jointly provided services. Authorities will need to take account of the adjustment processes of the industry in the way in which they apply their competition laws and policy. Otherwise, however, the Committee would anticipate that competition laws and policies should be applied in the same way in the context of local bus services as in any other sector.

CHAPTER 1

THE ROAD TRANSPORT SECTOR

A. DEFINITIONAL QUESTIONS

31.   The road transport sector is important in all OECD economies.   It is
also a diverse sector. This report is not concerned with transport by private
motor car nor with taxis.   It covers freight transport by road and road
passenger services.

32.   Road freight transport may be divided into the long-distance and
short-haul markets. Although there is no internationally agreed threshold, the
long-distance market begins at around 100-150 kms in some countries but may be
as high as 300-400 kms in others (1).   There is a further basic structural
distinction between full truckloads (FTL) and less-than-truckload shipments
(LTL) and between carriers operating on their own account and those offering
transport services on a for-hire basis. According to statistics from the
European Conference of Ministers of Transport (ECMT), the carriage-for-hire
segment accounted on average for 65 per cent of total tonne-kilometres in 1986
in nine European countries, this share remaining virtually unchanged since
1970 (2).   One other category of industry participants of increasing
significance in road freight is that of freight forwarding firms whose business
consists of undertaking the entire transport operation from pick-up to
delivery, co-ordinating the various operators who perform the different tasks
(e.g. pick-up, line-haul and delivery) and who consolidate small loads of
freight into one load to be carried by any mode.

33.   When taxi services and private motor cars are excluded, the road
passenger transport sector can conveniently be divided into two -- long
distance (or inter-city) bus (or coach) services and local bus services (often
municipal bus services).

B. ROAD FREIGHT

Statistical Background

34.   The road freight transport industry forms a significant activity in all
OECD countries, employing a large number of people and accounting for a
significant share of gross national product.

35.   Since the fifties there has been a spectacular growth in road freight
transport largely at the expense of the railways and despite a slight slowdown
after the oil shocks of 1973 and 1979. This growth has been highly correlated

with the general performance of the economy as measured by GNP. Between 1979 and 1982 for a sample of 16 OECD countries road freight increased at an annual average rate of 1.25 per cent, compared with a decline in rail and waterways freight (-0.80 and -0.42 per cent respectively) (3). For European Member countries (4) road freight traffic grew by 2.1 per cent in 1983 and 1984, by 1.3 per cent in 1985 and by 4.6 per cent in 1986. In 1986, road freight accounted for 63 per cent of total freight (road, rail, inland waterways and pipelines) in ECMT countries compared with a share of 56.3 per cent in 1975 and 46.8 per cent in 1965 (see Table 1). Rail's share has correspondingly declined from 33.9 per cent in 1965 to 18.9 per cent in 1986.

TABLE 1

MODAL SPLIT OF TOTAL FREIGHT TRAFFIC IN 15 EUROPEAN MEMBER COUNTRIES
(number of tonne/kilometres 1965-1986)

Mode	1965	1970	1975	1980	1981	1982	1983	1984	1985	1986
Rail	33.8	29.8	24.2	21.7	20.9	19.9	19.6	19.9	20.3	18.9
Road	46.8	49.7	56.3	58.8	60.4	61.9	62.4	62.0	61.9	63.0
Inland waterway	14.0	12.5	10.9	9.7	9.5	9.3	9.2	9.3	8.7	8.9
Pipeline	5.3	8.0	8.6	9.8	9.2	8.9	8.8	8.8	9.1	9.2
TOTAL	100	100	100	100	100	100	100	100	100	100

Source: Statistical Trends in Transport 1965-1986, ECMT 1989, Table D, p. 22.

36. Trends in international traffic also show a spectacular growth in international road freight over the period 1965 to 1986 (see Table 2). The number of tonnes loaded for international road transport in 16 countries increased fourfold over this period, while the number of tonnes loaded by rail and inland waterway increased only slightly. As a result, road transport almost doubled its share of international freight in 21 years (see part B of Table 2).

TABLE 2

**TRENDS IN INTERNATIONAL FREIGHT TRAFFIC (tonnages loaded)
FOR 16 COUNTRIES* 1965-1986**

a) Index (number of tonnes loaded in 1970 = 100)

Mode	1965	1970	1975	1980	1983	1984	1985	1986
Rail	86.6	100	87.3	107.9	87.9	97.5	101.9	93.8
Road	73.1	100	141.2	210.3	235.0	250.6	258.4	281.5
Inland waterway	73.5	100	106.9	119.4	112.5	119.9	115.0	119.0
Maritime transport	67.9	100	112.2	157.2	175.2	186.0	195.4	194.1

b) Modal split (tonnes loaded) in percentage

Mode	1965	1970	1975	1980	1983	1984	1985	1986
Rail	38.2	34.4	27.7	27.1	22.7	23.4	24.2	21.6
Road	22.5	23.9	31.2	36.7	42.2	41.8	42.7	45.2
Inland waterway	39.3	41.7	41.6	36.2	35.1	34.8	33.1	33.2
TOTAL	100	100	100	100	100	100	100	100

* Austria, Belgium, Denmark, Finland, France, Germany, Greece, Italy, Luxembourg, Netherlands, Norway, Spain, Sweden, Switzerland, United Kingdom and Yugoslavia.

Source: Statistical Trends in Transport 1965-1986, ECMT, 1989, Table E, p. 25.

37. In Australia, road freight accounted for 76 per cent of all modes in 1981-82, a figure which has remained fairly constant over the period 1970-71 to 1981-82. However when measured by tonne/kilometre performed, road's share is much less, accounting for 27 per cent of total freight carried in 1981-82. This share has however increased from 20 per cent in 1970-71. The annual growth rate for road was 7.3 per cent more than double the corresponding

growth rate for other modes.   It appears that over the decade road and   rail have tended to gain at the expense of sea transport and that road is competing more successfully with rail in the longer distance movements (see Table 3).

TABLE 3

AUSTRALIAN FREIGHT TASK (a) BY MODE, 1970-71, 1975-76, 1978-79 and 1981-82

Mode	1970-71		1975-76		1978-79		1981-82	
Tonnes consigned	million	%	million	%	million	%	million	%
Road (year ended 30 Sept.)	720.5	79	756.4	74	912.6	78	950.1	76
Rail (government and non-government)	151.6	17	212.7	21	216.6	18	250.5	20
Sea (b)	39.9	4	48.1	5	48.1	4	43.5	4
Air (scheduled carriers)	0.1	-	0.1	-	0.1	-	0.1	-
All modes	912.1	100	1 017.3	100	1 177.4	100	1 244.2	100
Tonne-km	'000m	%	'000m	%	'000m	%	'000m	%
Road	27.3	20	36.7	18	48.1	23	59.4	27
Rail	39.0	28	57.1	29	57.6	27	64.8	29
Sea (b)	72.0	52	104.9	53	105.0	50	98.2	44
Air	0.1	-	0.1	-	0.1	-	0.1	-
All modes (a)	138.4	100	198.8	100	210.8	100	222.5	100

(a)   excluding pipelines and conveyors.
(b)   Changes in the annual collection of sea statistics, implemented in 1971-72 and 1980-81, mean that the 1970-71 figure is not directly comparable with later figures and the 1981-82 figure is not directly comparable with earlier figures.

Source: National Road Freight Industry Enquiry, 1984, Appendix E, Table E11, p. 408.

38.   In Canada, the market share of road transport industries -- for hire and private trucking -- accounted for over 50 per cent of total operating revenues in transport in 1985, while the share of rail, the nearest competitive mode, accounted for 30 per cent.   In 1986, the for-hire trucking segment accounted for $8.2 billion of operating expenses and the private segment a further $4.1 billion.   These figures understate the real magnitude of the industry since they only include for-hire carriers earning more than $100 000 annually and only include trucking within Canada.   As regards trends in for-hire trucking in Canada, the number of carriers more than doubled from 1976 to 1986 and operating revenues increased from $3 billion to $8.6 billion.

Structure of the Industry

39.   Although there are variations from country to country, the road freight transport industry is generally characterised by a large number of operators, the majority of them small firms, frequently one-man owner-driver businesses. Many of the latter are under contract to large freight forwarding firms or to larger fleet operators.

40.   Thus in Canada, both the for-hire and the private segments of the Canadian trucking industry appear to be relatively unconcentrated, with the largest ten firms accounting for only 19.3 per cent of total operating expenses in the for-hire segment and for 13.3 per cent in the private segment and the largest 100 firms for 45.7 per cent and 39.8 per cent, respectively.   A breakdown by provinces using various measures shows that carriers domiciled in the provinces of Ontario, Quebec and Alberta accounted for over 70 per cent of operations in the Canadian for-hire industry.   Industry concentration levels do not appear to have changed significantly over the period 1976 to 1986.   When measured by revenues, the ten largest firms accounted for 15.5 per cent of total revenues in 1976 compared with 15.9 per cent in 1985.   The figures for the 100 largest firms show a fall from 48.8 per cent in 1976 to 44.0 per cent in 1985.   In Sweden, over 60 per cent of commercial operators in 1987 were firms operating a single vehicle driven by the owner alone.   In the United Kingdom, over 60 per cent of road haulage operators had fleets of less than five vehicles in 1987.   In France, 76 per cent of firms in 1985 had less than five employees and accounted for 18 per cent of the market, and firms having less than 50 employees accounted for two-thirds of the industry's turnover.   In Germany, in 1986 a total of 8 829 firms operated on the market for long-haul transport and 41 777 firms were active in short-haul transport and a further 32 901 firms engaged in private haulage.   International road transport accounted for nearly 10 per cent of total road haulage in Germany.   In Ireland, there are about 2 500 private road hauliers.   In Australia, a 1983 survey indicated that there were about 22 000 single truck owner-drivers full time in both long-haul and short-haul markets.   Many of these operated as sub-contractors to fleet operators or freight forwarders which have a strong market position in Australia.   In Portugal, 90 per cent of firms have less than three vehicles.   In Spain, more than 98 per cent of carriers have five or fewer vehicles and the average number of vehicles per firm is 1.4.   In Denmark, one-man firms account for 81 per cent of the number of firms.

Factors affecting growth of road freight transport

41.   As the previous paragraphs have shown, despite two oil shocks and periods of low economic growth, road transport has increased its position in relation to other modes.   One important reason for this is the greater flexibility of road transport in providing a wide range of services for different types of products and over a broader geographical area than covered by the railways or by waterways.   Over short distances for non-bulk goods of high value road transport has a distinct competitive advantage.   Only over longer distances for bulk freight do the railways become competitive.   The road freight industry can also point to increased productivity and efficiency during recent years.   Between 1973 and 1979 costs fell by an average of about 3.5 per cent for domestic transport and by 4.5 per cent for international transport despite rising fuel prices (5).

42.   Another significant factor is the development of motorway networks. Technological developments have also been an important factor over the last twenty years.   Examples are the design and construction of the vehicles used, the way the freight is handled and data processing and communication techniques.   These and other developments have enhanced the competitiveness and efficiency of the industry.

Concentration and Economies of Scale and Barriers to Entry

43.   The data mentioned in the previous section indicate that the road freight industry, in the absence of regulation, is capable of supporting numerous competing firms.   That is, there is no evidence of natural monopoly since there would appear to be no significant economies of scale and economic barriers to entry are low in most segments of the market because of small capital requirements and minimal product differentiation.   This applies particularly to short-haul non-specialised freight and to the long-distance markets where it is relatively easy for carriers to enter or leave the industry.   It is here that most one-man businesses operate.   The situation as regards short-haul specialist road transport may be somewhat different due to the need for industry- or product-specific vehicles, e.g. ready-mixed concrete trucks and brick trucks, which make entry more difficult (6).

44.   Available statistics on concentration confirm that concentration is low in the industry.   In Canada, for example, the concentration ratio of the ten largest firms in the for-hire trucking industry showed no significant change over the last ten years, being 15.5 per cent of total revenues in 1976 and 15.9 per cent in 1985.   The share of the 100 largest actually fell from 48.8 per cent in 1976 to 44 per cent in 1985 (7).   In the United States during the period 1979 to 1983, the share of total revenues held by the four largest freight carriers in the area of truckload traffic fell by almost 50 per cent. However there appears to have been an increase in concentration, measured by revenue, in the less-than-truckload sector.   Over the same period, the largest four in this sector increased their share of total revenue from 26.4 per cent to 30.6 per cent, though evidence indicates that this increase was due to expansion by the carriers concerned into new markets rather than increasing their share in their current markets (8).

45.   In the freight forwarding sector, concentration appears to be relatively high in some countries. In Australia, for example, the largest four operators accounted in 1982-83 for 35 per cent of all inter-state traffic moved by road and 71 per cent of that by rail. Since 1975, 79 firms have been acquired by the three major forwarders in Australia. In Sweden, about 80 per cent of sales on scheduled long-distance traffic are accounted for by two freight forwarding businesses.

C. PASSENGER ROAD TRANSPORT

46.   Public passenger road transport has two major components - inter-city bus (or coach) services and urban/suburban bus operations. There are in addition "other" services such as charter and tour services, school bus services and airport and taxi services. While not as large as the freight sector, passenger road transport still amounts to a significant economic activity. Reliable statistics are difficult to find for this sector but in terms of revenue or numbers employed the carriage of passengers by road appears to be between one-third and one-half of the significance of freight. Thus, in Canada, the for-hire bus services had total operating revenues of $3.4 billion in 1986 ($8.6 billion for road haulage). In Germany, for 1986, freight haulage amounted to DM27.7 billion of gross value added compared with DM9.35 billion for public passenger road transport. In Australia, the road freight transport industry in 1985 employed about 104 000 compared with 50 000 employed in passenger bus transport, excluding government bus operations.

Structure of the Industry

47.   In most countries road passenger transport as a whole is fragmented, consisting of a large number of operators with vehicle fleets of varying sizes. Thus the industry is relatively unconcentrated in general. The Australian Bus and Coach Association, representing private operators, claims that the industry comprises about 3 400 companies, operating approximately 14 000 buses and coaches. The smallest size category of firm (with four or less buses) accounted for 29 per cent of the industry and largest firms (with 50 or more buses) for 5 per cent. In Sweden, as of 1st January 1988, commercial passenger transport by road was handled by about 1 400 firms owning 12 000 buses. More than 90 per cent of these businesses were small entities owning at most ten buses.

48.   However, as regards inter-city road passenger transport the situation is more differentiated. In two countries - the United Kingdom and the United States - intercity services are highly concentrated. In the United Kingdom, the dominant carrier, National Express, accounted for 95 per cent of total coach passenger revenue in 1984 (the last year for which figures are available), while in the United States, the two largest carriers, Greyhound and Trailways (which have since merged), accounted for more than 70 per cent of Class I intercity industry bus revenues in 1980 (those firms with more than $3 million annual revenues). In France, inter-city bus services appear less concentrated with the largest three firms accounting for 20 per cent of the market. Urban transport is more concentrated in France with the largest three firms having 63 per cent of urban bus operations.

49.   Unlike freight transport which is largely in private ownership, there is a significant amount of public ownership in the passenger sector in most OECD countries, especially as regards urban bus services which are typically operated by local authorities. In addition, where local bus services are not operated directly by local authorities, many privately run services are subsidised by such authorities.

50.   As regards the growth trend in road passenger traffic, there has been a slow expansion between 1965 and 1985 in 15 European countries. Public road transport in terms of passenger kilometres increased by 74.5 per cent between 1965 and 1985 and by 54.5 per cent since 1970. However, despite this, public road transport has not increased its market share of total passenger traffic (including private cars, taxis and rail) owing to the even greater growth in the private motor car sector.   Thus the share of coaches, buses and trolley buses of total traffic declined from 15.8 per cent in 1965 to 11.3 per cent in 1986 (9).

CHAPTER 2

REGULATION AND DEREGULATION OF ROAD TRANSPORT

Introduction

51.   Both the road freight and passenger transport sectors are or have been
extensively regulated in OECD countries as regards conditions of entry and
exit, prices and routes to be operated. However, unlike the air transport
sector where deregulation only got under way in the late 1970s, several OECD
countries began 20 to 25 years ago to question the justification for detailed
regulation of the freight sector and, more recently, of passenger transport and
to begin reducing the extent of regulation of entry ("quantity" regulation)
which grew up in the 1930s when the motor vehicle market began to expand.

52.   There are 13 countries which have significantly deregulated the road
freight sector, i.e. by abolishing or reducing quantity or capacity controls or
rate-fixing requirements in the sector. These are Australia, Belgium, Canada,
Denmark, France, Ireland, New Zealand, Norway, Portugal, Sweden, Switzerland,
United Kingdom and United States. Several of these countries have done so
relatively recently. However, the extent of regulatory reform varies, with
Australia, Sweden, Switzerland, the United Kingdom and the United States
appearing to be the countries where deregulation has gone the furthest. Four
countries have fairly long experience: Australia (since the mid-50s -- although
the extent of deregulation varies from State to State), Switzerland (since
1960), Sweden (since 1964) and the United Kingdom (since 1968).

53.   Fewer countries have deregulated passenger road transport services which
remain therefore in most countries subject to extensive regulation and public
ownership.   The two exceptions are the United Kingdom, where there has been a
significant liberalisation since 1980 , culminating in complete deregulation in
1985 outside London and Northern Ireland as well as a splitting-up and
privatisation of the dominant firm, and the United States, since the enactment
of the Bus Regulatory Reform Act of 1982.

54.   This chapter will outline the shift in policy-makers' thinking on the
merits of regulating road transport and then describe the regulatory regimes
which currently apply in Member countries.

Arguments For and Against Regulation

55.   The main reason for the regulation of road haulage would appear to have
been the fear in the 1930s on the part of the regulated railway industry of
unfair competition from an expanding and unregulated road haulage industry.
The advent of competition in the form of lorries and buses eroded the profits
of the railways. The railways claimed that road hauliers would attract the
railways' most profitable business by lowering their rates while they (the

railways) would be prevented from retaliation because of regulation. Thus the view was favoured that there should be co-ordination between the transport modes requiring administrative guidance. The trucking industry also supported regulation by claiming that an unregulated road haulage industry would lead to intense competition that would be destructive and unsafe, forcing trucking firms into bankruptcy and resulting in men and vehicles being dangerously overdriven.

56.   Another generally held justification for regulation was the "public interest" rationale for regulation under which the public service nature of the industry was emphasised -- that shippers or passengers in small communities would lose service or be required to pay higher rates or fares than those in major traffic areas and that the public interest would best be served by regulation of a network of services permitting cross-subsidisation from profitable to unprofitable routes.

57.   The stimulus to deregulation of road freight transport came from several sources. An early move to partial deregulation in Australia in the 1950s came from a constitutional test over the division of regulatory power between the Federal and state governments, resulting in the abolition of certain federal regulations concerning inter-state transport.

58.   Later, studies pubished in the 1960s and 1970s in the United Kingdom and United States examined economic regulations in the light of their objectives to produce a stable, safe and profitable industry operating in the public interest. These studies found that control of entry and prices had not had these desired effects but did impose substantial costs on society.

59.   In 1965, the Geddes Committee in the UK found no evidence that a system of quantity regulation had contributed to road safety and felt that the system, by restricting the number of operators below free market levels, had actually reduced the efficiency of the industry by raising the price of transport and thereby the final price of goods (10).

60.   Various studies in the US found evidence of high prices and profits in trucking. In 1974, the US Council on Wage and Price Stability estimated the value of operating authorities (licences) at $3-4 billion (11) while Moore estimated the excess profits generated by licensing at $1.5 - $2 billion in 1972 (12). A comparison of profit rates in the 1970s showed that large general freight carriers consistently earned higher rates of return on equity than the average manufacturer (13). Excessive service competition was found in one study leading to empty backhauls of general freight vans 38 per cent of the time (14). Moreover, comparisons between regulated and unregulated trucking in the US suggested lower rates in the unregulated markets. A study of trucking in New Jersey, where intra-state shipments were not regulated, found that intra-state tariffs were generally 10-13 per cent below the interstate tariff for comparable shipments (15).

61.   Several US studies have also cast doubt on the alleged positive effect of regulation on stability in the trucking industry. In the late 1970s, i.e. before deregulation, mergers were taking place at the rate of well over 300 per year and this did not increase after deregulation (16).

62.   These studies provided some of the intellectual underpinnings for the movement to reshape the then pervasive economic regulation of motor transport.

63.   More recently, governments have been concerned about the environmental effects of road transport. Environmental concerns have led to such measures as the regulation of vehicle sizes and the creation of noise and exhaust emission standards to reduce the external costs of the industry. Environmental concerns have also led to regulation to affect the balance of freight moved by various modes of transportation, e.g., between road and rail.   Increasing road congestion will likely lead in the near future to further efforts to regulate in one way or another road usage, possibly by user charges or other such methods   to cause users to pay for the congestion they create.   Such environmentally motivated regulation is beyond the focus of this report.

64.   Safety is another important continuing justification for regulation but, like environmental concerns, is not the real focus of this report. Safety has, however, long been used as a justification for economic regulation, as mentioned above. This report therefore considers in the following chapter the evidence on the asserted link between economic regulation and safety.

65.   Finally, it should be noted that the public interest or social function in providing transportation services to small communities continues to affect the regulation of road transport and leads some Member countries to rely on public   provision of certain services.   Others, however, have begun to experiment with ways to reduce the costs of providing such services.

66.   Set forth below is a description of the shifts in the economic regulation of road transport in certain Member countries. The following chapter will then present the actual economic effects of deregulation in countries where such information is now available.

Current scope of Regulation

67.   In almost all countries anyone wishing to carry freight must obtain a licence.   The conditions for obtaining a licence vary from country to country. In some countries prospective carriers must not only show that they are "fit, willing and able" to perform the service but also that the service is required for reasons of public convenience and necessity.   It is this second condition which forms the regulatory basis for limiting the number of licences and hence entry to the industry. The first criterion of professional competence is still generally the basis of award of licences but it is the second criterion which has been progressively abandoned in countries which have ceased to regulate the number of operators and the services they provide. Quality regulation, i.e. regulation of technical standards and safety, continues to be strictly applied in all countries.   In addition, national regulatory arrangements sometimes involve rate-fixing for freight transport.

68.   Passenger transport is also subject to a licensing system in all countries although the systems are   operated with varying degrees of liberalisation from country to country.   Quantity and price regulation continues to be operated in most Member countries. The following section briefly summarises the present regulatory systems in force in reporting countries, as well as current international regulations.

69.   In _Australia_, until the mid 1950s, road freight was strictly regulated by the individual states. This control varied from State to State but generally involved control of routes and commodities, licensing arrangements and measures to limit competition with rail. State regulations were applied to both intra-state and inter-state transport. Following decisions on certain constitutional matters in the 1950s, much of this regulation ceased with respect to inter-state commerce. However, States still regulate some aspects, for example, most States have some categories of intra-state freight which are reserved for the railways. Most of the existing regulation is of a technical nature and aims to maintain safety standards. The principal regulations having a direct effect on industry prices are those relating to road user charges -- mainly registration charges levied by the State for heavy vehicles and fuel excise levied by the Federal Government to raise revenue for general as well as road-related purposes. Another area of government regulation which affects industry prices and practices is the heavily regulated Australian labour market where wages are determined under various State and Federal Industrial Awards.

70.   As regards passenger traffic in Australia, all operations are subject to technical regulation which aims to maintain safety standards and to forms of economic regulation which vary from State to State. New South Wales has recently deregulated passenger services, subject only to a public interest test, following a trial period of deregulation of a number of busy routes where the effect of deregulation was examined in detail. The State of Queensland has also deregulated entry into long-distance passenger coach services as from June 1989.

71.   In _Belgium_, road freight haulage was significantly deregulated in 1987 when quality controls largely displaced existing quantitative controls for the award of licences. In order to obtain an operating certificate a carrier must satisfy four qualitative tests - have a business established in Belgium, professional competence, no criminal record and financial capacity. To obtain a general licence to operate at national level a carrier must have held an operating certificate and operated within a radius of 75 km from its place of establishment for at least three years as well as meeting the quality tests. Such licences may also be obtained by transfer subject to further conditions. Any holder of a national licence may also obtain an international licence subject to the same qualitative controls.

72.   As regards rates, the general rule is that rates may be fixed freely by individual hauliers for national deliveries. For international transport, complete freedom will also operate as from 1st January 1990 subject to cost guidance being given by professional transport associations.

73.   Passenger transport is still subject to considerable regulation. Regular and specialised regular services are operated directly or contracted out to private operators by the railway company SNCV and by different local transport corporations. Occasional services are operated by private carriers. As well as satisfying quality controls similar to hauliers passenger carriers are subject to fare regulation by the relevant ministry for domestic services while fares on international services are agreed with the other countries operating the services.

74.   In _Canada_, the economic regulation of for-hire intra-provincial trucking falls   under   provincial   jurisdiction.   As   well,   the   regulation of

extra-provincial trucking has been delegated to provincial transport boards for many years.

75.   During the 1980s a series of events culminated in the enactment of the Motor Vehicle Transport Act of 1987. This legislation modified the terms under which the federal government delegated responsibility for the regulation of extraprovincial trucking to the provinces.   It has led to the reform of the regulation regarding entry and price control into the intra and extra-provincial trucking industry.

76.   One major objective of the Act was to liberalise entry requirements by changing the standards for licensing. Under the Act the federal government has delegated the discretion to license inter-provincial trucking to provincial motor transport boards. The Act provides that once the applicant's fitness is established, the requested licence will be issued unless an interested person objects.   The onus is then on the objector to provide the board with evidence that satisfies the board that, in the absence of evidence to the contrary, the operation of the extra-provincial truck undertaking in respect of which the licence is sought would "likely be detrimental to the public interest".   The board holds a public hearing only when this prima facie case is made, in which case the onus rests on the objector to establish public detriment.   The Act specifies that in applying the public interest provisions "a provincial transport board shall give primary emphasis to the interests of users of transportation services".

77.   Other than this latter requirement, the Act does not define what constitutes "public interest". However, on 1st June 1989 the federal cabinet issued a "Statement of Public Transportation Policy" which identifies a number of factors that a board may consider in determining whether detriment to the public interest is likely to result. The current "reverse onus" policy will cease to have effect on 1st January 1993 but before then the Minister of Transport will review its operation and may continue it. After the reverse onus policy ceases to have effect, entry will be deregulated except for the requirement to be "fit, willing and able".

78.   The second major objective of the Act was to eliminate rate control of extra-provincial trucking. Thus the Act has removed the obligation to publish or obtain approval for extra-provincial trucking rates.   Such rates are therefore now completely deregulated.

79.   In addition to action at federal level, many provinces have recently reformed their regulation of intra-provincial trucking, particularly as regards the reverse onus test for applicants, while others are attempting to introduce legislation on the lines of the 1987 federal Act.   Filing and regulatory approval of rates continue to be required in almost all provinces. However, only two provinces actually prescribe rates. Thus, in most provinces, rates are set by the carrier but are subsequently subject to regulatory approval.

80.   As regards the motor coach industry, three main federal Acts are aimed at economic control and safety. They are: the Motor Vehicle Transportation Act, 1987 (MVTA); the National Transportation Act, 1987 (NTA); and the Motor Vehicle Safety Act (MVSA).

81.   The NTA outlines the role of the federal government in transportation. Part IV of this Act provides for federal control over extra-provincial motor vehicle transport. However, the NTA only applies to extraprovincial motor vehicle operations which are exempt from the provisions of the MVTA. For the most part, all extra-provincial motor coach operations are subject to the provisions of the MVTA.

82.   Under the NTA, the National Transportation Agency (Agency) is given the authority to license extra-provincial bus undertakings pursuant to a public necessity and convenience test, to designate both areas served by carriers and the schedules to be followed, as well as to determine routes and toll charges. However, only the Roadcruiser bus service in Newfoundland is at present subject to this direct regulation by the Agency. Authority for the regulation of the rest of the Canadian bus industry rests with the provinces by virtue of delegation to provincial transport boards pursuant to the MVTA.

83.   For bus operations regulated by the provinces, new entry is rare because of a strictly applied public convenience and necessity entry test. This is true for both intra- and extra-provincial operations and regardless of whether jurisdiction was originally with the province or subsequently delegated. The only exception to this is found in the province of Alberta where, since 1st May 1987, "fit, willing and able" rather than "public need and convenience" has served as the test for entry into the intra-provincial charter bussing industry. Exit and re-entry into provincially regulated markets by incumbent carriers through transfer of authority is relatively easy. Rate filing is generally required but carriers usually enjoy broad discretion in setting and modifying rate structures and levels as they see fit. Urban bus operations, under municipal regulatory jurisdiction, are not subject to the terms of the NTA or MVTA.

84.   Provincial boards generally specify intra- and extra-provincial bus routes, capacity, service quality, safety standards and insurance requirements. Intra-provincial rates are officially regulated in all provinces except British Columbia, Saskatchewan and Manitoba. Bus parcel express rates are filed or prescribed in most provinces except Alberta, Quebec and Prince Edward Island. In each province only scheduled operations are permitted to offer bus parcel express. As well, in most provinces the right to operate a charter service is granted coincident to the grant of the right to operate a scheduled service.

85.   In Denmark, the road freight sector was regulated until the end of 1988 by the Road Freight Transport Act of 1973.

86.   With effect from 1st January 1989, the Danish road freight sector has been extensively liberalized. The 1973 Act which had regulated the issuing of licences, determined freight routes and established a system of approval of freight rates, was repealed.

87.   According to the new Act on Road Freight Transport (Statute No. 851), passed by Parliament on 21st December 1988, the quantitative regulation of ordinary road haulage has been repealed, as experience had shown that the previous scheme was unsuitable for regulation of road haulage.

88.   A licence is still required to operate as a haulage contractor, and such licence will be issued by the Road Haulage Council if the applicant has the requisite qualifications as listed in the Act.

89.   As from 1st January 1989 the road freight sector has been brought within the scope of the general competition rules (The Monopolies and Restrictive Practices Supervision Act 1955, as amended).

90.   As regards passenger transport, under the Bus Services Act, a licence is required for operating bus services, either from the local authorities or from the Danish Passenger Transport Council. The conditions are basically the same as for the conveyance of goods. The prices of scheduled services are controlled by the transport authorities but there is no price regulation of non-scheduled services.

91.   In _Finland_, the regulation of road freight has traditionally been comprehensive and dates from 1919. The basic conditions for awarding licences are that there is a public need for an additional service as well as the fitness and competence of the applicant. In examining the need for a new entrant, among other things, the trade association in question is asked for its views. Licences are then granted by the Ministry of Transport and Communications. The rates are fixed by the authorities for specialised services and for consignments weighing less than five tons in scheduled traffic.

92.   In 1988, the Ministry of Transport and Communications began a review of the "public need" requirement for awarding road freight licences. As a result of this, in 1989 a proposal was drafted for a new Freight Transport Act to take effect as from 1991. In accordance with the proposal, demand analysis, i.e. examining whether the applied service is needed for reasons of public interest, will be abolished. The basic requirements for obtaining a licence will then be the same as in EC Directive No. 74/561, i.e. good repute, appropriate financial standing and professional competence.

93.   In 1989, a proposal was also submitted for a Public Transport Act, which is proposed to enter into force in 1991. The intention is that, as a general rule, scheduled coach services will be financed by carriers through fare revenues, and the traffic will be subsidized only to the extent to which the authorities wish to maintain particular services that are not commercially viable. The services will be protected by the transport licence, but, along with profitable services, the carrier will have to operate unprofitable services as well. For the bus services provided or contracted out by the largest towns, competitive bidding will be introduced. Taxi licences will continue to be granted on the basis of demand analysis, but the system will be extended. In 1988, the licence regulation for charter traffic by coach was relaxed to promote competition.

94.   In _France_, road freight transport is regulated by the Act on Inland Transport of 30th December 1982 and by the Decree of 14th March 1986. In order to operate as a short or medium-haul carrier an applicant must be registered in the register of road freight carriers maintained by the local Prefects. This registration is subject to proof of professional competence - either a relevant diploma or passing a specific examination or three years' experience working in a transport firm. A certificate of registration permits transport of goods within the short or medium-haul zones which usually correspond to the area of

ten Departments (within a radius of 150 km). It also authorises some long-distance services, i.e. anywhere within Metropolitan France provided that the total weight of the vehicle used does not exceed 7.5 tonnes.

95.   There are three classes of licence for long-distance freight transport:

Class C - vehicles of less than 13 tonnes total weight
Class B - vehicles of less than 26 tonnes total weight
Class A - all other vehicles.

96.   Since the issuance of a decree in March 1986 there is no longer a limit placed on the number of licences issued. On the other hand, the licences cannot be transferred unless the business itself is also transferred. Moreover, the authorities decide in accordance with general transport policy and local needs whether to issue further licences.

97.   In 1986, the national quota system for licensing long distance freight transport was also reformed to allow entry on the basis of regional requirements. This led in 1987 to a considerable increase in the number of licences (+ 18 per cent).

98.   The profession of freight forwarder is subject to a separate licence and deposit procedure but to no special professional fitness requirements.

99.   Until 1st January 1989 road freight transport in France was subject to a mandatory tariff system which was provided for in 1949 legislation but which was not brought into effect until 1961. Freight rates were agreed by the National Road Committee (CNR) composed of carriers and approved by the Minister of Transport. The regulated rates applied to the transport of shipments of more than three tonnes and over more than 200 kilometres' distance with some exceptions such as perishable commodities and special forms of transport. Minimum and maximum rates were fixed for each route and type of goods within which the carrier was free to set his prices.

100.   The different operators in the road transport market are not all subject to the mandatory rate system. The functions of grouping together shipments and of operating city offices concerned with delivering individual shipments are not subject to regulation. An attempt was made by the transport associations to issue indicative rates but there were abandoned after an unfavourable opinion by the Technical Commission on Combines and Dominant Positions in 1976 (see Chapter 4). On the other hand, freight forwarders are subject to two restrictions: shipments of more than three tons are subject to the mandatory rate system and the freight forwarder's commission must not exceed a certain percentage (usually 15 per cent) of the price to the customer.

101.   The mandatory rate system was ineffective because individual carriers did not respect the regulated rates. Under Article 58 of Ordinance No. 80-1243 of 1st December 1986, the legal basis for the mandatory rates system for road freight was repealed with a transition period until 1st January 1989. However, the Ordinance does allow the National Road Council to set reference rates to guide particularly the smaller transport firms which do not always have the means of calculating their costs precisely. Only the National Road Council may

publish such rates; publication by another party could be challenged under the cartel law.

102. Passenger transport in France falls into two categories: urban and non-urban segments. Non-urban includes regular public services, charter public services, private services and occasional services. Private or occasional services can be operated by private firms. On the other hand, urban and interurban bus and coach services whether scheduled or non-scheduled are organised solely by the public authorities. The 1982 Act confers upon the Departments the main task of organising inter-city passenger services. The Departmental authorities draw up and keep up-to-date the Departmental Plan which contains the routes and services which have been authorised. The actual operation of these services may be carried out by the Department directly or by private firms contracted to do so. There are various types of contract but in all types fares must be approved by the organising authority. The contract may also involve subsidies by the authority to the private firm to the extent that the authority wishes to maintain particular routes or services which are not commercially viable.

103. Urban transport is the responsibility of local authorities who may either operate the services directly or contract them out to a private firm. Within the urban area the authorities may impose a specific transport tax on any firm with more than nine employees to help finance local services. The local authorities have also the task of approving fares for scheduled local services. Inter-city coach and bus fares are also subject to control.

104. In Germany, the Road Haulage Act of 1983, amended in 1986, provides the regulatory framework for road haulage. Private haulage requires no authorisation. However commercial haulage does require a licence for which applicants must meet requirements of reliability, professional competence and financial capacity. For long-haul transport, i.e. greater than 50 kms from the company's headquarters, an authorisation must be obtained. These authorisations are strictly limited in number -- there is a limited number of quotas for both general long-haul transport and for long-distance local haulage (up to 150 kms from the company's place of business).

105. There is also strict control of the rates charged for short-haul and for long-haul for-hire transport as well as a special rate for removal services. Minimum and maximum rates apply. The price actually charged is usually at the lower end of the scale. Government-set rates are laid down by rates commissions which, except for long-haul transport, are composed of representatives from both sides of the market. Within the rates commission for long-haul transport, consignors have only a consulting function. The rates set by the commission require government approval and are set in a binding manner by regulation. In the transport of merchandise imported and exported by way of sea ports, special rates may be arranged. Private transport is not subject to rate control. The carriage of goods on behalf of third parties is, however, prohibited, even between related firms.

106. An authorisation must be obtained for the paid or commercial carriage of passengers in motor vehicles, street cars, and trolley buses, both in the form of regular and occasional services.

107. Regular transport refers to regular services between a fixed point of departure and a final destination, allowing passengers to enter and leave the vehicle at certain stopping points. The authorisation for regular services may only be issued if, in addition to the personal reliability and professional competence, the safety and efficiency of the carrier have been guaranteed.

108. Before an authorisation is issued, the public interest in having such services established is considered. The authorisation is refused if:

-- the needs can be satisfactorily met by existing services,

-- the services applied for would cover transport tasks already carried out by existing carriers or railroads without providing a significant improvement of transport conditions,

-- existing carriers or railroads that provide such transport are willing to extend their own services.

As the result of these regulations, in the Federal Republic of Germany there are a number of concessions for the operation of certain routes by single companies.

109. Certain basic obligations have been imposed on operators of regular services; these are:

-- the obligation to operate the routes as authorised,

-- the obligation to transport passengers,

-- the obligation to charge fares according to the established rates.

Five forms of occasional transport may be distinguished:

-- excursions

-- vacation travel

-- travel by hired bus

-- taxi transport, and

-- travel by chauffeured cars.

Since taxi transport touches on important interests of the public, demand is considered to a limited extent. By contrast, in the case of the other forms of occasional transport, authorisations are issued when safety, efficiency, reliability, and professional competence have been established. For these forms of transport, there is no obligation to operate the routes authorised, to transport passengers, or to charge fees according to any fixed rates schedule.

110. In Greece, road freight transport is subject to licensing which covers both private and for-hire carriage. National freight rates are regulated by means of maximum and minimum rates but international transport rates are freely negotiated. Public passenger road transport is closely regulated as regards

numbers of buses and fares. New buses are licensed for carriage if there is a need for further services. At present, the number of buses is considered adequate for present demand.

111.   In Ireland, access to the domestic road passenger market is regulated by the Road Transport Acts, 1932 and 1933. Private bus operators are required to hold licences for scheduled road passenger services where a separate charge is levied for each passenger. Genuine private hire arrangements (such as a bus hired by a group for an all-in charge) are exempt from the licensing requirements. The key criterion in considering the grant or refusal of licences to private bus operators is the statutory requirement to have regard to the passenger road services and other forms of passenger transport available to the public on, or in the neighbourhood of, the route of a proposed service. The effect of the 1932 and 1933 Acts was to protect the railways. As a result of the restrictive nature of the legislation, relatively few licences have been issued to private bus operators. The Government has approved proposals for updating the legislation, with a view to more flexible arrangements for the licensing of private but operators.

112.   Since 30th September 1988, access to the profession of road freight haulage operator is governed by a system based purely on compliance with EC requirements. Any person, partnership or undertaking wishing to operate a road haulage business, using vehicles over 2.5 metric tonnes unladen weight, must hold a carrier's licence. Carrier's licences are unrestricted as to area of operation, type of goods carried or number of vehicles operated.

113.   In Japan, entry, rate and capacity regulations exist in the road freight and passenger sectors. Any applicant wishing to enter the general motor carrier business requires a licence from the Minister of Transport. Such licences are granted if the following requirements are met: the proposed service is in line with the demand for transport services and the new service will not bring about an imbalance between capacity and demand. The licence is granted for a particular route, area and kind of business.

114.   In addition, all freight charges and passenger fares must be approved by the Minister of Transport, taking into account in particular that the rates and fares charged are reasonable and include a reasonable profit margin, that there is no discrimination against particular passengers or shippers and that the charges or fares would not cause undue competition with other carriers.

115.   Any alternative in the services offered or number of vehicles operating also requires approval.

116.   Two bills designed to substantially relax entry, rate and other regulations in the freight sector were introduced in the Diet and passed in 1989.

117.   In New Zealand, all operators of road freight or passenger services who operate for hire or reward as well as all rental operators are required to hold a transport licence. Operators using vehicles exclusively for purposes other than hire and reward (known as "own-account" operators) are exempt from transport licensing. Each vehicle owned by a licensed operator (except rental vehicles) requires a Vehicle Authority which is issued freely to those who apply. Licensed operators must pay an annual fee per vehicle registered.

118. Applicants for licences are required to supply details concerning the proposed operation as well as an estimate of the operation's anticipated expenditure and its financing. Licences are then issued by the appropriate Transport Licensing Authority with all decisions made by this body being subject to appeal to the Transport Licensing Appeal Authority. Once a licence has been issued it has an indefinite life: revocation or restriction of a licence is possible, however, under Sections 140 and 141 of the Transport Act 1962.

119. In 1983 the Transport Amendment Act came into force, introducing into transport licensing the principle of qualitative licensing. This Act saw the abolition of all geographical restrictions on road transport operators; restrictions on road transport competition with New Zealand railways removed; entry into the industry became a question of the applicant's suitability rather than a bureaucratic assessment of demand for the respective services. Rate-fixing became a matter to be decided solely between operators and their customers.

120. These steps have led to a gradual transition from quantitative licensing to qualitative licensing -- the emphasis now moving to the applicant's ability to demonstrate that the proposed service will be "safe and reliable".

121. In Norway, as of 1st January 1987, the system of licensing for road freight transport was liberalised. Licences are still required but a special permit for scheduled services is no longer required. Licences are not geographically limited and the notion of licensing a particular route was abolished. Licences are now awarded on objective grounds. Licences are no longer required for acting as a transport intermediary, for freight forwarding businesses and for certain specialised services.

122. Tariff approval has ceased to exist since 1984. Under the Price Act, maximum tariffs may be laid down and are still in force for taxis.

123. Since 1981 the county authorities have overall responsibility for bus services, including the fixing of fares. For routes crossing county borders fares are subject to approval by the Ministry of Transport and Communication. For these routes, the Ministry of Transport and Communication also issues the licences.

124. Norwegian regulation is also characterised by the existence of significant subsidies for passenger transport. In February 1989, the Ministry of Transport appointed a committee to evaluate the usefulness of competitive tendering in local passenger transport which is seen as a way of securing the more efficient use of public subsidies.

125. In Portugal, road transport rates and fares were significantly liberalised in 1986 by a decree/law of 17th December. From that time all freight hauliers became free to set their own rates for domestic transport. They remain subject to the reference rates for international transport laid down in the relevant EEC regulations. Passenger transport which is considered a public service operated under Government licence, except for those services run by local authorities, is subject to price control, with the Ministries of Prices, Transport and Finance (for publicly-owned enterprises) being involved in the price-setting process.

126.   Regular freight services as well as inter-city bus services are subject to licensing. The former constitutes a small and declining part of the market.

127.   In <u>Spain</u>, under the Act on Land Transport of 1987, the authorities are empowered to fix obligatory or reference tariffs for road transport, whether passenger or freight, scheduled or non-scheduled. At the present time, the system of obligatory tariffs is applied to both passenger and freight transport, except as regards short distances (less than 200 kms) and as regards freight transport in lightweight vehicles. These last-mentioned segments of the market are thus entirely free of price control.

128.   The   Land Transport Act also established   the principle of free competition in land transport. However, the Act provides that access to the market may be restricted by the authorities if there is an imbalance between supply and demand, if an increase in supply of services would be likely to cause an imbalance, if capacity needs to be adjusted, if general economic reasons exist related to a better use of resources or if the transport system as a whole is in danger of being perturbed.

129.   In fact, the non-scheduled transport of passengers or of goods has been completely liberalised as regards local services. Quantity regulation still applies to the road transport of passengers over longer distances in vehicles with more than nine seats and to the long-distance national transport of goods in heavy vehicles. As regards scheduled passenger services, licences are awarded to individual carriers.

130.   In addition, carriers are subject to the conditions required under Community   regulations: financial capacity, reliability   and professional qualifications.

131.   In <u>Sweden</u>, under the commercial traffic legislation that has been in force since 1st January 1980, licences are necessary to transport goods and passengers by road on a commercial basis.   Applicants go through a process called   fitness testing, in which they must   meet certain criteria of professional knowledge, financial condition, law-abiding conduct, disposition to discharge obligations towards the general public, and other circumstances of importance.

132.   In addition, before 1st July 1989 permission to run local passenger services had to satisfy a test of necessity, which is to say that the intended traffic had to be deemed to be necessary and otherwise convenient. Licences to carry on such transport were awarded for defined routes or within a specific traffic area, and with use made of specified capacity. Operating licences could   be revoked.   The licensing authority was the respective county administrative board (a regional civil service department, as opposed to the county   councils, which are politically   elected bodies).   There is   a corresponding   central authority, the Transport Council, to deal with inter-regional scheduled services.

133.   As from 1st July 1989, licences are still required to operate commercial road freight and passenger transport services. However, the publicly owned county traffic organisations no longer need a special licence to operate scheduled bus services. These bus services are to some extent usually financed by the local and regional authorities. The county traffic organisation is in a

position to tender for services in competition where scheduled-service licences previously conferred a monopoly on the licensee. However, some of the public traffic organisations own bus enterprises and this has effects on tendering.

134. Applicants for traffic licences still have to satisfy the same basic fitness assessment. The necessity testing of contract-hire and scheduled traffic by bus is discontinued. However, if a long-distance scheduled bus service is to be sanctioned, the intended traffic must be found not to harm established railway traffic or the mass-transport service which the county traffic organisation is operating. On the other hand, licences must be awarded if the applicants make it seem likely that the provision of bus services would be considerably improved.

135. Prior to 1st April 1987, persons applying for licences to operate scheduled road freight services, or to forward carriage of goods by lorry, had to satisfy the authorities that there was need for their proposed services (necessity testing). During the 1970s the same sort of testing had been abolished in stages for different types of road freight transport. During the 1960s, moreover, the awarding of licenses had been gradually liberalised.

136. In 1972, the state ceased to concern itself with the fixing of maximum rates or charges for or road freight transport. Maximum rates for scheduled long-distance bus traffic were not fully abandoned until January 1989. Where municipalities and county councils continue to be responsible for and largely finance the local and regional bus traffic, these bodies still set the prices that are charged.

137. In some regions there are tendencies towards increased public ownership of bus traffic firms; in other regions, municipal bus traffic services have been privatised.

138. Within a closely related commercial traffic category, taxi services, a decision has been taken to implement deregulation measures beginning on 1st July 1990, on which date rates regulation and necessity testing will expire.

139. In Switzerland, a licence to operate regular road passenger services is required but road freight transport does not require a licence.

140. As regards passenger transport, an applicant for a licence has to fulfil two conditions -- he must provide proof that there is a need for the service he proposes and the existing public transport network must not be subject to significant competition from the new service. Until the end of 1986, fares required approval but with the entry into force of the Public Transport Act on 1st January 1987, public transport enterprises are free to set their own prices subject to the possibility of intervention by the Confederation in the event of abusive fares.

141. Road freight transport has been completely deregulated since 1960. There are no controls over entry or rates. Thus any person may enter the industry subject only to the restriction on the maximum size of vehicle permitted - 28 tons.

142. It should be stressed, however, that Swiss transport policy is characterised by concern for environmental protection, favouring transport by rail over longer distances rather than by road and public transport rather than private, as shown by the subsidies given by the Federal government and by the cantons to maintain and operate public passenger transport. Similarly, in relation to freight transport, the government encourages combined road/rail traffic by subsidising investment and operating costs for this type of transport.

143. In the United Kingdom, both road haulage and road passenger transport have been extensively deregulated, whereby the former system of quantitative licensing in both segments has been replaced by qualitative controls.

144. Quantity controls were removed from the road haulage industry by means of the Transport Act 1968 which followed a report in 1965 of a committee chaired by Lord Geddes, set up to examine the state of the industry. The Committee concluded that the main objectives of any licensing system were the promotion of public safety and efficiency in road transport operations. The Committee found no evidence to support the idea that a system of quantity regulation had contributed to road safety whilst they felt that by restricting the number of operators it had actually reduced the efficiency of the industry by raising the price of transport and thereby the final delivered price of goods. A system of "quality licensing" was however recommended, making the granting of a licence dependent on safety standards subject to the licence being revoked if operators did not maintain the condition of their vehicles.

145. Following the Geddes report, a system of quality regulation was instituted by the Transport Act 1968 under which applicants for a standard national or international operator licence must satisfy the Licensing Authority of their good repute or fitness and of their financial standing. The Licensing Authority also takes into account the vehicle maintenance arrangements and the suitability of the proposed operating centre. In 1984 new legislation empowered Licensing Authorities to take into account environmental effects.

146. Under the 1968 Act, hauliers are free to compete on price and quality of service as there are no pricing controls. The only remaining form of regulation is thus confined to ensuring legal and safe operations.

147. The Transport Act 1980 began the deregulation of road passenger transport. That Act abolished the controls over routes, stopping places and fares exercised by the Traffic Commissioners. There remained, however, a system of licensing introduced in 1977 whereby applicants for a public service vehicle licence (PSV) have to satisfy the Traffic Commissioner that they are of good repute and sound financial standing and have proper arrangements for keeping vehicles in good mechanical order. Buses and coaches have to be inspected annually by official vehicle examiners who can prohibit the use of unsatisfactory vehicles.

148. The 1980 Act removed quantity restrictions from regular express coach services of over 30 miles and from long-distance excursions and tours. The 1980 Act also began the deregulation of local bus services by changing the criteria for awarding a road service licence (RSL). Up to then, if there were an objection to an application for an RSL, the applicant had to convince the Traffic Commissioner that it was in the public interest to grant the RSL. The

new Act changed the burden of proof so that an RSL had to be granted unless it could be shown to be against the public interest. The Act also provided for "Trial Areas" within which the RSL system would be completely suspended. Three areas were designated by local authorities.

149.   Experience in the Trial Areas was one reason why the Government decided to proceed to full-scale deregulation of local buses in the Transport Act 1985. The 1985 Act also reduced the 30-mile express coach limit under the 1980 Act to 15 miles.

150.   The 1985 Act also provided for the abolition of the RSL system outside London and Northern Ireland. Operators merely have to register details of their services with the Traffic Commissioners. There is no right of objection. The Traffic Commissioners may only modify registrations by attaching a condition to the operator's licence if the Local Traffic Authority asks them to impose a Traffic Regulation condition on grounds of congestion or road safety and the Commissioners agree that such a change is necessary.

151.   In parallel to the deregulation of freight and passenger transport in the United Kingdom, an extensive programme of privatisation and dismemberment has been undertaken. Following the privatisation of the National Freight Consortium in 1982, the National Bus Company was split up into 72 operating companies and privatised between 1986 and 1988. There have subsequently been several mergers between these companies and between them and independents. The Scottish Bus Group is also about to be privatised. In addition, deregulation is to be extended to London in the early 1990s and, in anticipation of this, London Buses Limited has restructured itself into eleven smaller units which were established as subsidiary companies in 1989. There are no plans to privatise the company at the present time. London Regional Transport is also extending the procedure of competitive tendering of bus routes. It is envisaged that the percentage of services put out to competitive tender will increase from its current level of 25 per cent to 40 per cent by 1992.

152.   In the United States, freight motor carriers are regulated by the Inter-state Commerce Commission (ICC) under the Inter-state Commerce Act. Until the mid-1970s, regulation under the Motor Carrier Act of 1935 limited competition by, in effect, establishing a presumption against new entry or expansion. In addition, all motor carriers' rates were subject to ICC approval and most were established by rate bureaus, which were associations of motor carriers that set rates collectively with antitrust immunity.

153.   The Motor Carrier Act of 1980 drastically altered the ICC's regulation of non-passenger motor carrier rates. Although the Act requires that rates be filed with the ICC, the Act provides that the ICC may not suspend, revise, or revoke an independently established rate on the ground that it is unreasonably high or low if filed under a "zone of ratemaking freedom" and if it is not more than ten percent higher or lower than prior rates defined according to specified statutory benchmarks. The ICC has limited authority to change these percentages after taking into account the state of competition and other factors.

154.   The 1980 Act also changed the scope of antitrust immunity accorded to rate bureau activities. Since 1st January 1984, carriers no longer have had antitrust immunity for the collective discussion and setting of specific

single-line rates. Subject to certain procedural safeguards, however, immunity continues for collective discussion and setting of general rate increases or decreases after that date, provided that discussions are limited to industry average costs rather than to individual markets or particular single-line rates. Immunity also remains for commodity classification changes, tariff structure changes, and several non-price rate bureau activities.

155. With regard to entry, the 1980 Act requires an applicant for new or expanded authority to prove the existence of a "public need" for the authority and to prove that it is "fit, willing and able" to provide the service. Opponents of applications for new authority must show not merely that they would be injured by a diversion of traffic, but that the public interest would be adversely affected by the granting of the new authority. Though the exact meaning of these legal criteria and evidentiary requirements regarding the issuance of new authority under the Act is still the subject of debate and litigation, it is generally accepted that the Act has liberalised entry to promote greater competition.

156. In 1982, a moratorium was imposed on the issuance of certificates of authority to foreign motor carriers of contiguous countries that substantially prohibit grants of authority to persons of the United States to provide motor transport. There are no other restrictions on entry by nationals of other countries.

157. The Bus Regulatory Reform Act of 1982 enacted a similar regulatory scheme for motor carriers of persons. The US bus industry, especially the giant carrier Greyhound, actively supported this regulatory reform, unlike the US trucking industry which was opposed to deregulation. The 1982 Act, however, fell somewhat short of total deregulation. The changes include a removal of authority for collective setting of single-line rates effective 1st January 1983, and a similar termination with respect to joint line rates effective 1st January 1984. The Act also allowed greater pricing flexibility for bus carriers by creating a pricing zone within which carrier's can set fares without Interstate Commerce Commission (ICC) interference. In addition, the Act reduced state control over intrastate rates, service, entry and exit by interstate bus companies. However, state control generally remains over petitions by bus operators to raise fares or to enter or exit markets.

158. The Act made it easier for both regular-route and charter carriers to enter the industry. Applicants for charter services have only to meet safety and insurance standards. Foreign motor carriers of passengers, however, are subject to the certificate of authority moratorium noted above.

159. Antitrust immunity was retained for general fare increases, broad tariff restructurings, and promotional and innovative fares advanced by the industry as a whole. Antitrust immunity was also abolished for collective rate making on single-line rates in 1983 and on joint-line rates in 1984.

160. Federal regulations protect private charter bus carriers from possible unfair competition from subsidised local carriers. These regulations provide, with certain exceptions, that local carriers may not use equipment or facilities subsidised by the federal Department of Transportation to offer charter service in competition with a private firm.

161. In the _European Communities_, regulation and liberalisation of road transport must be viewed in the context of the development of a common transport policy and the creation of a single market in 1993.

162. For the transport of goods, market access is regulated by a system of quotas on the number of licences issued both at national and Community level. National licences, which represented about 50 per cent of European traffic in 1987, are negotiated on a bilateral basis and are valid for a one-way journey between the two States concerned. Community licences (16 per cent of all traffic in 1987) are valid for the whole territory of the EEC and for an unlimited number of journeys. The EEC Council determines each year the total number of Community authorisations and how they are divided up among the different States. It is planned to increase the number of Community licences by 40 per cent per year for the coming years with the aim of abolishing them altogether on 1st January 1993. At that date, entry to the sector will be regulated solely by qualitative criteria.

163. In 1989 a Council Directive strengthened the qualitative criteria for entry to the sector, fixing the minimum conditions to be fulfilled with regard to integrity, financial capacity and professional capacity.

164. Up to 31st December 1989, the prices for the transport of goods by road between Member States were fixed by a Council Regulation of 1st December 1983. This Regulation gave Member States the possibility of opting either for a system of reference tariffs (amounting to price recommendations) or for a system of mandatory tariffs. In 1988, the Commission submitted a draft Council Regulation which received the Council's approval, establishing complete pricing freedom as from 1st January 1990.

165. In order to allow competition to develop in an even-handed setting, important provisions have been adopted in three areas:

- fiscal harmonization
- social harmonization
- technical harmonization.

In the fiscal area, the Commission has drawn up

- a draft directive relating to excise duties which deals particularly with taxes on motor fuel; and

- a draft directive concerning taxes on vehicles which is designed to harmonize such taxes and establish collection of the taxes by the States within which the journeys are made.

166. In the social area, in 1988 the Commission proposed an amendment to the Council Regulation of 1985 relating to harmonization of certain provisions of a social nature, particularly driving hours. Since the application of this Regulation has given rise to difficulties of interpretation, simpler procedures are proposed as well as a directive to introduce common control procedures.

167. As regards technical harmonization, a new Directive was adopted by the Council in 1989 fixing the weights, dimensions and other characteristics of road vehicles.

168. In 1985, the Commission also transmitted to the Council a draft Regulation fixing the entry conditions for non-resident carriers to domestic road haulage markets of Member States (cabotage). This Regulation was adopted by the Council in December 1989 and will enter into force on 1st July 1990. From that date, any road haulier established in a Member State, through a system of cabotage quotas and subject to certain conditions will be allowed to carry out national road haulage operations in a different Member State from the one in which he is established. In the event of a crisis due to the introduction of cabotage, the Commission is authorised to take the necessary measures.

169. There has been some liberalisation of the transport of passengers by bus and coach between Member States. Occasional services as well as transport provided by a firm for its own employees are exempt from authorisation. Shuttle, regular and regular specialised services remain subject to authorisation.

170. In 1987, the Commission issued a draft Council Regulation which would simplify the system of authorisations for international passenger transport by coach. This proposal would extend the exemption from authorisation to shuttle services which include accommodation. These services would be authorised to make four stops to pick up or set down passengers in the countries of departure and destination and a maximum of 30 per cent of passengers who have effected the outward journey would be allowed to change groups.

171. Also in 1987, the Commission submitted to the Council a draft Regulation fixing the conditions for cabotage services in passenger transport by coach. This proposal is designed to allow authorised carriers to undertake the international transport of passengers and, if they have a genuine link with a Member State, to operate national transport services in a Member State other than where the carrier is established.

172. As in the case of road haulage, quality criteria for access to the profession of passenger road transport carrier were strengthened in 1989.

Other international rules

173. The European Conference of Ministers of Transport has issued a number of Resolutions and Recommendations in the road transport area. Most of the Resolutions and Recommendations concern technical and safety aspects relating to national and international transport, such as weights and dimensions of vehicles, speed limits, seat belts, road signs and traffic lights with a view to harmonizing standards. Some are concerned with the education of road users and with standardization of training for driving licences as well as with social problems related to driving, especially drink (17).

CHAPTER 3

THE EFFECTS OF ROAD TRANSPORT DEREGULATION

174. As noted in Chapter 2, relatively few countries have had a long experience with deregulation of road freight transport and even fewer with regulatory reform in passenger road transport. This chapter will therefore focus on those few countries where sufficient time has elapsed to attempt an assessment of the effects of deregulation as well as giving some preliminary evidence in countries which have recently begun to deregulate. The analysis is also limited by the availability of evidence or studies on the effects of deregulation in the countries concerned. The countries dealt with are Australia, France, Norway, Sweden, the United Kingdom and the United States as regards freight transport and the United Kingdom and the United States for passenger road transport. Some information on two countries more recently into the field - Canada and New Zealand - will also be mentioned.

AUSTRALIA

175. Economic regulation of inter-state road freight has been minimal since the 1950s. Real freight rates have fallen considerably and consistently for many years and the quality of service is generally regarded as very high. Evidently, the long period of time that has elapsed since deregulation precludes any conclusions as to what extent the deregulatory process has contributed to the improved performance of the road freight sector or whether these positive effects would have occurred anyway.

176. However, there are segments of the market where participants exercise a significant degree of market power. The main example of this is in the freight forwarding sector where the major freight forwarders exercise strong bargaining power in the purchase of line-haul services from both road haulage subcontractors and from the railways. This situation contributes to continued instability among long-distance owner drivers and small fleet operators in the line-haul road freight market. Instability is particularly severe in a pool of about 800-1 000 subcontractors (18).

177. While the short-haul market appears generally to perform efficiently in meeting the needs of users, it may be adversely affected in some circumstances by private restrictions on entry, in particular "closed yard" arrangements (in the specialist sector) under which associations of providers of freight services and associations of buyers agree to limit entry to particular workplaces. This practice appears to be common in the brick cartage industry in Australia. Brick manufacturers engage subcontractor owner-drivers to operate from specific brick yards thus forming a cartel restricting entry by other prospective carriers. The right to work out of the yard becomes therefore business goodwill which may be sold to newcomers for considerable sums (19).

178.   The beginning of deregulation of road freight in Australia can be traced to two legal actions in New South Wales in 1954 and 1955 which successfully challenged the constitutional validity of State regulation of interstate transport of goods (20). On the basis of these judgments State legislative control of interstate goods transport was virtually withdrawn. As a result of this freeing, there was an influx of new operators into the industry which led to unrestricted competition not only between road operators in interstate transport but also between road and rail on inter-state routes.

179.   While the process of deregulation of freight traffic on intra-state routes began in the 1960s it proceeded slowly. Exemptions from "rail preference" for particular categories of freight were gradually granted to allow road transport to compete for the movement of certain commodities and/or the use of specific routes. However, certain categories of intra-state freight, e.g. grain and coal, are still reserved to rail in some States.

180.   As mentioned in Chapter 2, Australian experience with deregulation of intrastate road passenger services is more limited. Only two States - New South Wales and Queensland - have deregulated intrastate passenger services. In New South Wales, deregulation followed a six-month trial period of liberalisation of several busy routes which gave rise to a detailed examination of the effects.

181.   As regards the trial period of deregulation from 17th November 1986 to 17th May 1987 in New South Wales, the overall assessment was that the market for intrastate bus services was highly competitive over the two trial corridors (Sydney-Canberra and Sydney-North Coast) characterised by reduced bus fares, ease of entry and exit, availability of similar technology to all operators and absence of predatory pricing.

182.   The two corridors were chosen because of parallel rail links in New South Wales. Prior to the commencement of the trial, one passenger bus company on each route held the licence to operate express bus services, e.g. between Sydney and Canberra, and on the Sydney-North Coast corridor, between Sydney and Port Macquarie, and between Sydney and Ballina.

183.   Of the twelve bus operators who provided services during the trial period, three were granted permits to operate over both corridors, one was granted a permit to provide services over the Sydney-Canberra corridor, and eight operators were granted permits to provide services on the Sydney-North Coast corridor.

184.   For the purpose of the trial only express bus services were allowed to operate on the Sydney-Canberra corridor. On the Sydney-North Coast corridor bus operators were required to transport passengers over a journey of at least 160 kilometres, and were not granted pick-up and set-down rights for passengers travelling solely between Sydney and Newcastle.

185.   The major beneficiaries of the trial were the travelling public. The trial stimulated competition between bus operators on both corridors resulting in fare reductions and expanded services. Bus fares were reduced by $5 on the Sydney-Canberra corridor and by about $10 on the Sydney-North Coast corridor at the commencement of the trial. Despite increases during the trial, fares were still lower at the end of the trial than prior to its commencement.

186.   Compared with the same period twelve months earlier, demand for bus
services during the six-month trial on the Sydney-Canberra corridor increased
by over 80 per cent and on the Sydney-North Coast corridor by more than 130 per
cent.   It was estimated in the study that 52 000 bus passengers were diverted
from other modes of transport on the Sydney-Canberra corridor and 31 000 on the
Sydney-North Coast corridor. In addition, generated bus trips during the trial
were estimated to be 8 000 and 10 000 on the respective corridors.

187.   The major "disbenefit" arising from the trial was the significant impact
that bus services had on the revenue flows of competing modes of public
transport over both corridors. The estimated fall in rail passenger revenue on
the Sydney-Canberra corridor was $433 000 and the Sydney-North Coast corridor
$399 000.   The loss in revenue to regional airlines over the two corridors was
estimated at $247 000 and $471 000 respectively.

188.   Despite these losses in revenue, neither railway nor airline management,
except East-West Airlines, responded to either price or service competition
emanating from the bus companies during the six-month trial. Towards the end
of the trial period East-West Airlines offered a 40 per cent discount on air
fares on the Sydney-North Coast corridor.

189.   Analysis of the market structure for bus services during the trial
revealed that, on the Sydney-Canberra corridor, two of the four bus operators
providing services dominated the market, carrying around 80 per cent of
passengers between them.   On the Sydney-North Coast corridor, patronage was
more evenly distributed among the operators. Over this corridor, eight of the
original ten operators shared nearly 90 per cent of the market.

190.   On the Sydney-Canberra corridor over 70 per cent of bus passengers paid
full fare for their journey during the trial. In comparison, 55 per cent of
rail passengers travelled by some form of concessionary fare.   On the
Sydney-North Coast corridor an estimated 54 per cent of bus passenger paid full
fare, whereas 70 per cent of rail passengers travelled by concessionary
fares (21).

191.   In the case of Queensland, intra-state passenger bus services
deregulation in June 1989 only applied to entry. However, while there has been
an increase in the number of licences for different services there has been no
increase in the number of operators.

CANADA

192.   As mentioned in Chapter 2, with the coming into force of the new Motor
Vehicle Transport Act, 1987, on 1st January 1988, entry control into the intra-
and inter-provincial trucking industry has been substantially relaxed. In
addition, rate control of inter-provincial trucking was abolished. However,
some of the underlying trends and structural shifts apparent during the first
years of deregulation constitute a continuation of developments which emerged
prior to the formal enactment of regulatory reform measures. A notable example
of this is the continued rationalization and consolidation of the Canadian
trucking industry.

193. Deregulation has led to increased competition in both the truckload and less-than-truckload (LTL) segments of the industry, while the sources of this increased competition are different for each sector. The reduction of entry controls resulted in many new entrants in the truckload segment of the market which, except for some specialized operations, has a relatively low entry capital threshold. The LTL sector was rather marked by the expansion of routes and services of established regional carriers. Increased competition brought lower truckload rates, particularly in the high volume general freight markets in Quebec and Ontario. Though subject to discounting in some market segments, LTL rates were more stable as on-time performance and service reliability were the major factors of competition in this sector.

194. Despite generally good economic conditions, the financial performance of the Canadian trucking industry in the first post-deregulation years was not as favourable as during the previous five years. In some cases, this situation was the result of adjustments arising from pre-deregulation developments and, in other cases, it was related to revenue losses concomitant with loss of traffic or rate erosion from increased competition. To remain competitive, carriers have increased their emphasis on marketing, and placed greater importance on customizing services to shippers' requirements. Large general freight carriers have also tended to diversify into specialized services such as expediting small parcels.

FRANCE

195. In France, although freight transport was not fully deregulated until 1st January 1989 when the obligatory tariff system was abolished, partial liberalisation of the licensing system was begun in 1979-80. At that time the licensing of short-haul transport and for rental of long-distance transport was abolished and the mandatory tariff system for long-distance freight transport has since been applied only to distances above 200 km (22).

196. This partial liberalisation had the effect of increasing the number of licences and thereby the potential supply of freight transport services with demand not keeping pace, but this trend had been apparent since 1976. Competition on rates was extensive: despite the existence of the obligatory tariff system, prices, especially for international goods transport, fell below the floor rate.

197. Since 1985, growth in the goods transport sector increased substantially but at a lower rate than the increase in the number of transport authorisations, 17 per cent as against 25 per cent during the period 1985 to 1987. Over a longer period (1974 to 1987) the number of transport authorisations doubled but traffic increased by only 9 per cent (23).

TABLE 6

PRICE OF ROAD FREIGHT TRANSPORT IN FRANCE

(Annual percentage change)

Year	1983	1984	1985	1986	1987
Domestic transport					
- short-zone	11.6	5.1	12.2	6.1	- 6.4
- long-zone	11.3	7.4	2.8	0.6	- 3.4

Source: Girault, see note 22.

198.   Table 6 shows the trend in prices of road freight transport in France
and for international transport engaged in by French hauliers over the period
1983 to 1987, bearing in mind that the quota system was liberalised in 1986,
with a 15 per cent increase in authorisations allowed. This appears to have
had an immediate impact on price levels which fell by 6.4 per cent for
short-zone traffic and by 3.4 per cent for long zone. It should be noted that
the short-zone prices, which were completely deregulated as regards prices and
licences, showed a greater fall than the long-zone traffic, which was still
subject to some regulation. It is noteworthy also that the prices of
international transport have been more stable than for domestic transport. One
of the main reasons for this would appear to be the greater competition from
the entry of small hauliers with less than five employees into this segment of
the market (24).

199.   Employment in road freight increased by almost 20 000 from 1984 to
1987 (25).

NEW ZEALAND

200.   As mentioned in Chapter 2, all controls on route, area and price for the
road freight transport industry were abolished as from 1st November 1983 and
there was a general phasing out of rail restrictions for freight operators,
thus bringing road and rail into direct competition. As a result the road
transport industry has generally seen an increase of new entrants and a
widening in the range of services offered. Consumers have generally benefited
from the increased competition and improved marketing of freight services.
Rail has suffered as a result of deregulation, the primary impact being seen in
a downturn in revenue. The amount of rail freight carried has also decreased
and the distances over which that freight has been carried have shortened. It
should be noted, however, that deregulation has not been the cause of this
downturn, for the trend was well in existence before deregulation came into

45

force.   Only an indirect link between deregulation and an acceleration of this trend in rail freight can be demonstrated.

201.   Deregulation has generally led to an increase in competition within the road transport industry. There has been a significant increase in the numbers working in the licensed goods service industry, a rationalisation of the heavy goods   service   fleet,   general   increases   in   road   freight   employment opportunities, distances travelled and diesel use in the road sector and greater competitiveness with rail. All have signalled greater capacity and activity in road transport than would in general be expected from economic growth alone since 1982-83.

NORWAY

202.   Since complete deregulation of road haulage only took effect in 1987, there has been little analysis of its impact. However, one important initial effect has been the increase in the number of new entrants into the industry. There was an increase of 41 per cent in new licences issued in 1987 compared with 1986. The fact that hauliers may now compete with subsidised scheduled services resulted in 1987 in a reduction in the number of subsidised services by 12 per cent (5 per cent fall in the value of subsidies). This indicates that low traffic areas have lost service.   On the other hand, there are indications of stronger competition in high traffic areas since licences are no longer restricted to specified regions. New entry has apparently not resulted in over-capacity; capacity has remained at the same level as before deregulation, indicating some restructuring of existing firms (26).

SWEDEN

203.   As noted in Chapter 2, Sweden has progressively deregulated its road freight transport sector since 1964 (27). During the 1950s it was found that the regulatory system did not achieve the aims for which it had been set up. The railways were operating at a substantial deficit. The licensing system had fragmented   the   road   haulage   industry   into   many   submarkets and caused inefficient use of vehicles. It had also promoted the growth of monopolistic groups due to restrictive entry control.

204.   The effects of the relaxation of restrictive licensing is shown in a decrease in the number of licence applications refused. In 1964, 17 per cent of all applications -- from newcomers and from established hauliers -- were refused.   In 1968, the refusal rate was down to 1.5 per cent. While the rate then increased to 10 per cent in 1972, this increase was mainly caused by the introduction of a new criterion of economic suitability as a requirement for new entrants. It should be noted that the 1972 refusal rate was three times higher for new hauliers than for existing hauliers.

205.   During the ten-year period 1954-64, i.e. before liberalization, the total carrying capacity measured in tons within the road haulage industry increased by 11.8 per cent per annum. From 1964 to 1966 it jumped up to nearly 16 % per annum, although this great increase was a phenomenon of short duration.   From 1966 to 1968 it was down to 7.6 per cent per annum, and from 1968 to 1972 carrying capacity increased by only 5.5 per cent per annum.

206. It is worth noting that the long term growth of capacity was not affected by liberalization, even if the big increase in 1965-66 was no doubt due to the less restrictive capacity control. Changes in carrying capacity have primarily reflected general economic developments in the country.

207. The number of road haulage firms showed a rapid expansion during the first years of the new transport policy. It rose from 13 000 in 1963-64 to 18 600 in 1968-69, but the following years saw only a modest increase. This large increase has received much attention in the transport policy debate, but the competitive effect of this increase was to some degree lessened by the fact that existing but illegal operators took the opportunity to legalize their business. Also many drivers for existing own-account operators acquired their former employer's vehicle and became professional hauliers carrying the original traffic. New haulage firms were responsible for a relatively small part of the total increase in carrying capacity. According to estimates made, they were responsible for on the average about 25 per cent of the total capacity increase from 1965 to 1972.

208. Since the early 1950s, the large carriers have increased their share of the market and liberalization did not change this trend. Firms having at least eleven lorries increased their share of the total number of road haulage vehicles from about 9 per cent in 1953 to about 18 per cent in 1964 and to 26 per cent in 1974.

209. Own-account transport has declined considerably during the years of less restrictive licensing for professional hauliers. In 1961 carriers for hire or reward produced 60 per cent of the total number of ton-miles by road. This share increased to 64 per cent in 1966 and to 80 per cent in 1974. This development has received scant attention in the discussion on the results of the transition from restrictive to liberal licensing. The rapid growth of the road haulage industry has often been interpreted as mainly a transfer from rail to road. To a significant degree, however, shippers have chosen to hire professional operators instead of carrying the goods in their own vehicles.

210. The less restrictive capacity control did not change in any fundamental way the competitive position for the railways. Even if deregulation lowered the costs and the price level in road freight transport, this has had only marginal effects compared to the effects of changes in other transport policy measures affecting the relative price of road to rail. Because the prior quantity control of road haulage firms had been ineffective in protecting the railways, deregulation did not cause any serious diversion of traffic from the railways.

211. An important conclusion which was drawn from Swedish developments in 1981 was that deregulation - or at least partial deregulation - did not lead to permanent instability in the road haulage industry (28). During a transitional period there was, as expected, a large influx into the industry but after a short time the balance between supply and demand was restored. The less restrictive capacity control has given existing carriers a chance to expand their business more easily than before, and the medium-sized and large firms had increased their share of the market. Furthermore, liberal licensing had brought about a more effective use of resources within the industry, as detailed licence prescriptions in terms of the goods to be carried, the

customers to be served, etc. have been removed. The abolition in 1979 of territorial restrictions has had the same effects.

212. Concerning passenger transport, recent information on the economic effects of the new tendering systems used by county traffic organisations indicates that scheduled bus services in many counties will be procured at significantly lower costs than under the former licensed monopoly system.

UNITED KINGDOM

Road freight

213. As discussed in Chapter 2, the Transport Act of 1968 changed licensing criteria from quantity to quality. One of the most significant effects of the new licensing regime is the proportion of applications which are challenged. In the mid-1960s, 20 per cent of applications were challenged, the majority by existing hauliers. From 1968, only about 1 per cent of applications for operating licences were challenged each year, most of them by local authorities on grounds of unsuitable operating centres. More recently, the proportion of licences challenged has risen to over 7 per cent, mostly on environmental grounds introduced under the 1984 Act (29).

214. The threat of licence revocation is the ultimate sanction for the enforcement of safety and maintenance standards. Action is now taken each year in about 300 cases (less than 3 in every 1 000 operators) (30).

Development and Structure of Road Haulage

215. The rapid growth in road freight activity started before deregulation, freight carried by road doubling between 1958 and 1968, from 36 to 74 billion tonne kilometres. There has been a further 50 per cent increase to 109 billion tonne kilometres in 1987. The road share of total freight carryings grew from 55 per cent in 1958 to 87 per cent in 1987. Freight carryings by rail declined from 37 billion tonne kilometres in 1952 to 14 billion tonne kilometres in 1987, which was only 11 per cent of the combined road/rail total.

216. The number of heavy goods vehicles rose steadily from 443 000 in 1950 to a peak of over 600 000 in 1967. The number has since fallen by nearly 30 per cent to 435 000 in 1986 due in part to the use of larger lorries.

217. By 1986, articulated vehicles of 33 tonnes and over comprised 8 per cent of the total HGV stock and accounted for a third of the carryings. However, the overall capacity of the HGV fleet fell from a peak of about 4 million tonnes in 1965 to 3.5 million tonnes in 1986 while total freight carriage rose by a third during this period. Thus, there was an improvement in utilisation of about 50 per cent.

218. There has been little change over the last 25 years in the size of businesses. Throughout the period about 35 per cent of heavy goods vehicles have been in fleets of up to five vehicles and at the other end of the spectrum about 20 per cent in fleets of over 50. Over 50 per cent of operators have only one vehicle and 87 per cent have up to five vehicles.

Stability

219.   Prior to the 1968 deregulation, the road haulage industry argued that increased competition might lead to inadequate charges and profits producing many bankruptcies and declining standards of vehicle operation and safety. A Committee of Inquiry in 1978 (31) found no evidence of such effects and formed the impression that the road haulage industry was remarkably stable.

220.   The total number of operator licences rose to a peak level of around 140 000 between 1972 and 1975. The level fell in 1977-78 following the introduction of the "professional competence" requirement. Since 1978-89 the total has remained at about 130 000. Although the road haulage industry was affected by the recession in the early 1980s the number of licences issued in 1981-82 was only 4 per cent below the 1978-79 level.

221.   The rate of turnover amongst operators has also remained very stable. Every year since 1974-75 the number of new applications (as against renewals) has been about 10 per cent of the fairly constant total number of licences, and this figure is similar in all the Traffic Areas. The figures must be interpreted with some caution, since a new applicant may be a reconstituted company or someone who has previously operated in another Traffic Area. But one can deduce that the drop-out rate must have been of a broadly similar order to the new applications, although the disappearance of an operator from the market normally shows up only when his licence expires.

222.   The 10 per cent of operators who for various reasons do not renew their licences each year is very much larger than the number of bankruptcies. The latter has averaged about 640 a year (i.e. about 1/2 per cent of total operators) and even in the peak year of 1983 it was only about 1 per cent of operators. The Foster Committee in 1978 found that nearly half of a representative sample of operators had entered the industry before 1960, and only 4 per cent had entered during the last three years.

223.   Standard licences for hire and reward now amount to about 55 per cent of total operators, with international standard licences comprising about 11 per cent. This compares with the situation before 1968 when only 10 per cent of operators held A and B carriers licences and 90 per cent were "own-account". The proportion of own-account carryings, in tonne-kilometres, fell from 49 per cent in 1962 to 32 per cent in 1986. There has been an increasing tendency for user firms either to contract out their work or to use spare capacity in their own vehicles to carry goods for others.

Safety

224.   During a period of rapid growth and keen competition in road haulage the safety record of the industry has been good. The involvement rate of heavy goods vehicles in accidents has fallen by 60 per cent since 1968, compared with a fall of 37 per cent for cars. By 1986 heavy lorries were involved in only 66.1 accidents per 100 million vehicle kilometres, compared with an involvement rate of 118.8 for cars. This partly reflects the fact that 30 per cent of HGV traffic, compared with 20 per cent a decade ago, is on the motorways.

225.   The standard of vehicle maintenance, as reflected in the failure rate in the annual statutory tests, improved significantly in the early 1970s. The failure rate fell from 30 per cent in 1969/70 to 19 per cent in 1975/76 and has since remained fairly constant at around 20 per cent (32).

Costs and Prices

226.   A 1980 UK report (33) found some evidence of substantial increases in productivity in road haulage in the 1950s and these were reflected in comparatively stable road haulage rates in the 1950s and early 1960s when rail freight charges rose sharply. However more recently, hauliers' costs have risen rapidly. Almost all of this increase arose from increases in drivers' wages but fuel costs were little different in real terms in 1980 than in 1960.

Road Passenger Transport

a) Long-distance coaches

227.   The initial result of the 1980 Transport Act was an expansion in the number of long-distance services. In the first two years of deregulation, the State-owned National Bus Company (NBC) increased the number of inter-city services by 17 per cent and provided frequency increases on a further 55 routes. By 1983, nearly 700 new express coach services were in operation and the vehicle kilometres had increased from 90 to 138 million. There was a corresponding increase in the number of passengers carried. By 1985, the number of passengers carried by National Express, the long-distance subsidiary of NBC had increased by two-thirds, rising from 9 million in 1980 to 15 million in 1985 (34).

228.   This growth in long-distance coaching had a considerable impact on railway services. It has been estimated that the loss of passengers to coaches cost British Rail some £12 million in 1981 and £15 million in 1982 (35). The initial reaction by British Rail to increased competition by coaches was to make deep price reductions but this resulted in losses (overall, the Inter-city rail services lost £196 million in 1982). However British Rail then adopted a more flexible marketing strategy which resulted in an increase in traffic and reduction in losses (36).

Prices and Entry Barriers

229.   There was a marked impact of deregulation on fares. Table 4 shows some fares in constant pounds charged by National Express before and after deregulation. The period March 1980 serves as a baseline in Table 4, as this period was near the end of the regulated era. All fares were lower in May 1981 than in March 1980, reflecting the intense competition which broke out with deregulation. It was estimated by the Transport and Road Research Laboratory that there had been a 40 per cent reduction in real terms in the period following deregulation. The initial sharp drop in National Express fares shown by Table 4 corresponds with the creation of a new consortium called British

TABLE 4

SOME NATIONAL EXPRESS STANDARD PERIOD RETURN FARES FROM LONDON (£)

London to:	March 80	May 81	May 82	April 83	Oct. 84	April 86	Aug. 88
Birmingham	8	4	6	7	7	11	9.6
Bristol	9	5	8	8.5	8.25	10	11.5
Cardiff	11.5	7	8	10	10.5	12.5	16
Exeter	13.7	7	9	10	11	13	16
Leeds	13	10	10	11.5	12.5	15.5	19
Newcastle	19.25	13	13	14	16	19	19

Source: Department of Transport, September 1988.

Coachways, formed with the aim of establishing a new network of express services between the major cities and offering fares that were approximately 50 per cent of the fares of National Express before deregulation. Many smaller independent operators also entered the market. However the period of intense competition was short-lived. By 1983 the consortium had collapsed, and National Express prices have since risen sharply. The real fares shown in Table 4 average some 20 per cent higher in 1988 than before deregulation in 1980.

230. The main reason for the consortium's failure appears to have been the competitive response by National Express in lowering fares. There were also difficulties in creating the necessary infrastructure for operating the new services - creating terminals and making their locations as well as the location of pick-up and set-down points well known to passengers. Many of the other independent firms have also given up the struggle against the resources of National Express. However some 15 firms have survived by specialising in just one or two routes offering a high quality product (37).

231. The continued dominance of National Express was the unexpected outcome of deregulation of long-distance coaches in the United Kingdom. Thus, although it is believed that economies of scale are not significant in the industry, there would appear to be some entry barriers caused by the incumbent carrier's extensive network of services, agents and ability to advertise as well as its national timetable of services.

232. A further significant entry barrier would appear to exist in the ownership by the dominant carrier of the major coach terminals. Thus in 1985 the new Transport Act required coach stations to be opened to all operators. The impact of this change has not yet been studied in detail. It is however

thought that a fairly stable level of use has continued since 1985, National Express carrying around 15 million passengers per year (38). There appears also to have been much greater stability in the number of operators, turnover being much less than in the early post-1980 deregulation period. The most significant new service has been the opening of the "Oxford Tube" service between Oxford and London in 1987 with a high degree of frequency throughout the day.

Safety

233. Despite offering faster services by means of motorways, express coach services have had a good safety record since deregulation. Between 1980 and 1986 the accident involvement rate of coaches fell by 15 per cent, better than the rate for heavy goods vehicles and that achieved by cars.

Commuter services

234. Before 1980, due to opposition by British Rail, commuter coach services were effectively blocked under powers to object to licences for such services. Since deregulation commuter services to London have increased steadily. In 1980, there were only 60 coaches offering such services. This increased to 185 in 1983 and 340 in 1984. The current figure is probably over 400 although growth is now marginal. It has been estimated that they carried about 6 per cent of all BR commuter passengers in the Greater London area. It would seem that smaller operators have captured a significant share of this new market, gaining about 40 per cent of the total in 1983 (39), although the large public sector operators still obtained the major share of this new market.

235. As might be expected this growth in commuter coaching has been largely at the expense of BR as well as of the bus and underground services of London Regional Transport. However since 1986 a substantial fall has occurred in commuter and local traffic due to increased traffic congestion in London, improvements in rail services as well as doubts about the financial viability of peak hour coach services (40).

b) Local Bus services

236. Although the first steps towards deregulation of local bus services were taken under the 1980 Act when the burden of proof in licensing was changed, i.e. the onus was put on opponents of new entry, complete deregulation outside London and Northern Ireland took effect only in October 1986. Any assessment of its effects must therefore be tentative while the industry adjusts to the new situation. The complete deregulation of buses was preceded by a period of trial deregulation in three areas of the UK. Based on the experience in these three trial areas as well as on a Government White Paper in 1984, the conclusion was drawn that cross-subsidization was an undue burden on the declining number of profitable services, depriving travellers of a higher standard of service justified by their demand. It also concluded that there was a significant scope for greater efficiency which was not being realised because of the absence of competition. Local authority subsidies which had

increased thirteenfold from 1972 to 1982 in real terms were leaking into costs (41).

237. As well as ending the road service licensing system (see Chapter 2), the 1985 Act changed the basis for awarding subsidies for unprofitable services by putting them out to competitive tender. The National Bus Company was also split up into 72 separate companies and privatised. Privatisation was completed by March 1988. Municipal operations were not privatised but were set up as separate companies owned by their parent local authority and operated on a commercial basis.

238. The UK Department of Transport initiated an extensive monitoring programme following the adoption of the 1985 Act to establish its effects, the results of which have been published in a series of papers (42). This initial exercise has finished but monitoring is continuing on a wide, though less extensive scale.

239. While it is too early to draw firm conclusions after some three years' experience of deregulation and because of varying effects between areas, overall there was considerable growth in levels of service. The number of vehicle miles registered nationally increased by about 18 per cent between October 1986 and March 1989 (43). About 84 per cent of vehicle miles were operated commercially (i.e. without subsidy) in 1989. Thus there have been substantial savings in direct bus service subsidies, although these have been partially offset by increases in administrative and publicity costs to local authorities.

240. Fares in general do not appear to have been affected by deregulation, although the introduction of competition from new entrants has led to some fare reductions. In metropolitan areas there were substantial fare increases largely as a result of the bus companies charging realistic fares for their services due to the withdrawal of subsidies. In most areas there was no change or marginal improvements in concessionary fares. In most areas fare increases were broadly in line with inflation. A number of arrangements facilitating through ticketing and the use of pre-paid discount tickets have been terminated because services are run by different operators.

241. Changes in bus services have benefited some passengers and disadvantaged others. A survey of some 1 400 bus users in Scotland early in 1987 found that 15 per cent of users said that they used buses less often than before deregulation and only 9 per cent more. Since then, however, service levels have been increased and early organisational problems, especially providing adequate passenger information, have been largely overcome. In non-metropolitan areas, more bus users approved the changes than not and just over half felt that the quality of service was substantially the same.

242. About 450 more private operators are now running local bus services and over 60 per cent of services are now provided by private operators, compared with 8 per cent before deregulation. There has been a substantial growth in competition between operators on common routes.

243. The main innovation in local bus services since deregulation has been the introduction of minibuses, 7 000 of which were being operated in over 600 places in 1989. They represented 10-15 per cent of the total stock of

vehicles in use on local bus services. Frequencies of minibus services have been considerably higher than conventional services typically by a ratio of 3:1. These services have been popular with the public causing a considerable growth in patronage (44). However the long-term financial position of these services is not clear, given that the overall costs of operating a minibus service are likely to be approximately 60-90 per cent greater than those of a conventional bus service, assuming three minibuses to one conventional bus (45).

Safety and maintenance

244. Due to the short period since deregulation it is not possible to discern any change in bus safety and maintenance standards. Statistics on accident rates during the first two years will be available at the end of 1989.

UNITED STATES

The Effects of Road Freight Transport Deregulation

245. As mentioned in Chapter 2, the Motor Carrier Act of 1980 did not abolish all regulations of interstate trucking in the United States but considerably relaxed controls over entry, rate fixing, operating authority and carrier commodity restrictions.

Structure of industry

246. The most striking effect of the Act has been the growth in the number of road transport carriers and intermediaries. Between 1979 and 1985 the number of carriers almost doubled. Since 1980, over 20 000 new carriers have received operating authority and most existing carriers have expanded their operations (46). Most of this new entry was in the Class III category, i.e. the smallest firms with less than $1 million annual revenue. In addition, because most of the new entrants were small firms lacking the marketing skills and resources required for efficient operation, the easing of entry restrictions allowed an explosion of transport brokerage firms, i.e. intermediaries between shipper and carrier. The number of licensed brokers rose from 952 in 1982 to 5 908 in 1988 (47).

247. As in the case of airline deregulation, one result of eliminating routing restrictions has been the creation of hub-and-spoke networks for less-than-truckload (LTL) shipments. Shipments are consolidated at major terminals and sent to various destinations, thus enabling economies of vehicle size to be realised (48).

Costs and prices

248. It should be recalled that the 1980 Act drastically curtailed the power of motor carrier rate bureaus to set rates collectively but did not abolish the ICC's role in reviewing pricing. By creating a zone of rate freedom for pricing services, the Act allows carriers to raise or lower prices within,

initially, a range of 10 per cent per year but which was indexed to the producer price index after two years. Moreover beginning in 1984 the rate bureaus could not intervene in the establishment of single-line rates. This flexibility has enabled carriers to price much more independently and to simplify rate structures and tariffs in response to shippers' demands (49). Most of these rate changes have had the effect of exerting a downward pressure on prices. The generally held view is that there has been a considerable relative fall in prices since deregulation. One study obtained an annual average cost savings of $3.8 billion from 1981 to 1986 (50).

Revenues and Profits

249. A survey of earnings and traffic volume undertaken by the Interstate Commerce Commission in 1985 found that the net income of the largest motor carriers of property (general freight and specialised commodity hauliers) rose to about $450 million in both 1983 and 1984, compared to a net income of $177 million in 1982 (a recession year) (51). The net income of 100 of the largest general freight carriers improved substantially in 1983 compared with 1982 but declined in 1984. The general freight carriers did not perform as well as the specialised commodity carriers because of the increased competition from freer entry and discounting, and this may be a normal consequence of adapting to changed competitive conditions (52).

Wages and Employment

250. Data from the Bureau of Labor Statistics for the years 1978 to 1984 showed that the relative level of trucking industry employment was as favourable or better than manufacturing industry in each year from 1978 to 1980, 1982 and 1984 and slightly worse in 1981 and 1983. By 1988, the unemployment rate was slightly lower than the manufacturing average (53).

251. Following deregulation, trucking wages have declined relative to wages in other sectors. Since mid-1980, most of the new carriers have been operating with non-union drivers (54). It also appears that several trucking firms in financial difficulty negotiated separate contracts with the Teamsters under which employees accepted stock ownership in exchange for lower wages. Driver wages have increased since 1979 at about half the rate of US workers wages nationally. Trucking wages during the 1970s were about 25 per cent higher than manufacturing wages. However by 1987 they were only about equal to such wages (55).

Level of Services

252. One of the arguments against deregulation was that trucking services particularly to smaller communities would be reduced as unprofitable routes were closed down. However, the Department of Transportation has found that shippers were receiving in 1988 service that was as good or better than before deregulation (56). The number of competing carriers has increased and improvements in service quality have been reported many times more often than deteriorations, regardless of the shipper's or receiver's location (57).

Intermodal Competition

253. Deregulation of both trucking and railroads in 1980 has probably had its most significant impact in the area of competition between the two modes, particularly for full truckload or larger volume traffic. The existence of modern road networks in the US has meant that trucks can be competitive with railroads for even long-distance hauls (58). This has led the railways to develop extensive trailer on flat-car (TOFC) operations capable of reaching shippers located some distance away from the rail network. This added flexibility has led to a traffic growth in TOFC and container-on-flat-car (COFC) traffic (involving ocean cargo containers) of 70 per cent during the period 1981 to 1986.

Safety

254. While trucking has been partially deregulated from the economic standpoint in 1980, motor carrier safety was not deregulated. Indeed, the Department of Transportation has increased its safety monitoring and has found no valid statistical evidence showing a position relationship between economic deregulation and safety performance in the industry (59). Since 1980, three pieces of federal legislation have been passed to deal with motor carrier safety, involving in particular increased federal funds to states for on-road vehicle inspections, enforcement officer training and inspector training (1982 and 1984 Acts), and establishing a framework for the national licensing and policing of commercial drivers (1986 Act) (60).

255. Critics of deregulation have argued that increased competition reduces profits and forces trucking firms to operate at the lowest cost, thus reducing investment in new vehicles and forcing drivers to infringe safety regulations. Some have also argued that the increased influence of shippers in negotiations with carriers might lead to unsafe practices resulting from cutting rates.

256. According to data on accidents from the National Highway Traffic Safety Administration, however, accident rates have actually declined during the 1980s. While fatal accidents involving heavy combination vehicles remained at around 4 000 per year during the period 1976-1986, there was a significant decline in the number of accidents per 100 million vehicle miles from 6.6 fatal accidents per 100 million vehicle miles in 1976 to 4.6 million in 1986. Moreover this reduction has occurred despite an increase in the number of miles travelled (from 49.7 billion vehicle miles in 1976 to 82.7 billion in 1986) (61).

Inter-city buses

257. From the coming into force of the Bus Regulatory Reform Act of 1982 until 3rd August 1988, more than 5 900 applications had been filed by new and existing firms, 72 per cent by new applicants and about 14 per cent for regular route authority. The number of companies providing inter-city bus services rose from roughly 1 300 in 1980 to more than 3 500 in 1987. Total revenues rose only slightly to $1.96 billion in 1987, below the average 1981-86 revenue level. The ratio of operating costs to operating revenues worsened from roughly 94 per cent in 1980 to nearly 97 per cent in 1986 (62). From 1974 to

1984, Greyhound's ridership decreased by 40 per cent and profits were half the 1974 levels. Thus one of the main aims of the Act -- to improve the industry's financial condition -- has not been achieved. Profit margins have been reduced no doubt due to increased competition.

258. The largest carriers have established a number of discount fares, although fare increases have also occurred (63).

259. Bus companies have also benefited from reforms at the state level (the 1982 Act required the ICC to grant intra-state regular route authority on routes over which the carrier had inter-state authority if the carrier is fit, willing and able, unless the ICC finds that authorisation would not be in the public interest). As of August 1988 the ICC had received 62 petitions to review intra-state rates, most of which concerned intra-state fares which were lower than comparable inter-state fares (64).

260. Greyhound and Trailways used the 1982 Act's provisions to discontinue or reduce services to numerous points in their intra-state network, although few of the smaller carriers have reduced services (65).

261. It should be noted that most of these scheduled services that were abandoned were to small communities (those generating less than 50 passengers a day), continuing and accelerating a trend that had already begun before deregulation. The number of communities receiving bus service declined on average by 3.3 per cent per year from 1975-1982. Following the passing of the 1982 Act, this decline increased to an average of 9.2 per cent from 1982-1983 and to 11.6 per cent from 1983-1984 (66). In some states the rate of abandonment has been much higher. In Illinois, for example, 27 rural counties lost service between 1982 and 1985 (67). It would therefore seem that new entry has not occurred in services to small cities.

262. The segment of the market that has benefited most from deregulation is that of charters, where there has been a large increase in new entrants. According to one study (68), 1 706 applications (88.4 per cent of all applications) were for charter authority in the first year of deregulation, 764 by existing firms and 942 by first-time applicants. This represented a 500 per cent increase over the average of the previous five years. The increase would appear to have been at the expense of the smaller traditional bus companies operating both scheduled and charter services (69), thus exacerbating the loss of regular bus services in rural areas.

263. It should be noted that the growth of charter and special services at the expense of regular services was already apparent in the 1970s, i.e. before deregulation. Between 1970 and 1977, the earnings of the largest carriers in the sector increased by 177 per cent to amount to 15.2 per cent of large carrier revenue. Thus deregulation appears to have continued a trend that was already apparent in the intercity bus sector, though regular route service remains the most important source of revenue. A 1983 study of the bus industry cost structure indicated that the lowest costs were achieved by a mixture of regular, charter and bus package express services (parcel delivery services by bus) (70).

264. In the United States, the scheduled bus industry has not participated in the general growth of passenger travel largely because of increased private

motor car usage and discount air fares. In May 1988, the deteriorating financial condition of the second largest passenger carrier in the US, Trailways, led the ICC to approve the merger between the two largest companies - Greyhound and Trailways (see Chapter 4 for further details).

265. It should be added that the inter-city bus industry continues to be at a disadvantage compared with its air and rail competitors. The price of petrol has remained relatively low in the 1980s, thus encouraging private motor car travel and, following deregulation of the airline industry, price competition has been intense with many air fares undercutting bus fares in long-haul markets. In addition, Amtrak continues to receive substantial federal assistance, making it a substantial competitor in some markets.

Innovation

266. One of the hoped-for developments since deregulation has materialised, namely the operation of rural "feeder" operations, using vans to provide services where full-size buses are not warranted by demand and bringing passengers into the main network hubs operated by Greyhound. In addition, the use of linkages with other modes of transport, particularly airports, has been noted in some areas. The profitable future of the US inter-city bus industry would seem to depend on the further development of these innovations.

DISCUSSION

a) Road freight transport

267. Regulatory reform initiatives undertaken in Australia, Canada, France, New Zealand, Norway, Sweden, the United Kingdom and the United States have had broadly similar and highly beneficial results. These benefits, discussed in more detail below, include increased entry, lower prices, more efficient use of equipment and higher employment.

268. The benefits of deregulation, however, do vary across countries. As Chapter 2 has indicated, there are two main reasons for the lack of uniformity: the varying extent of regulatory reform in the countries concerned and the length of time that has elapsed since the reform was instituted. In Denmark and Ireland, deregulation occurred so recently that results are not yet apparent. In the geographically larger OECD countries such as Australia, Canada and the United States, the situation is further complicated by the differing levels of deregulation at state or provincial level compared with federal level. Inter-state haulage is completely deregulated in Australia and is almost totally deregulated in Canada and the United States but there remain a number of significant regulations in force at the state or provincial level.

269. Considerable amounts of new entry have occurred wherever licensing has been liberalised. In Norway, for example, new licences increased by 41 per cent in the first year following deregulation. Likewise, in Sweden, the number of road hauliers increased sharply, from 13 000 to nearly 19 000, in the first five years following the liberalization of licensing policies. Significant new entry also occurred in Australia, France, New Zealand, the UK and the US.

270. Deregulation has not always led to increased capacity however. The increased efficiency following deregulation may result in more goods being carried in fewer vehicles. This occurred in the UK, for example, and utilisation there increased by 50 per cent following deregulation. Such improved utilisation can be explained, inter alia, by the new freedom of carriers to haul goods on return trips, reducing empty backhauls, and reduced own-account carriage.

271. Prices generally fall following deregulation even if capacity does not always rise. In France, for example, prices dropped sharply following deregulation. Moreover, rates in France dropped the most in short-haul traffic, where liberalization was greatest. In the US, savings from lower prices have been estimated at almost $4 billion annually.

272. Rail transport has generally suffered from the increased attractiveness of road transport, but this trend away from rail to road is a long-term one which existed before deregulation, as discussed in Chapter 1, and may only have been accelerated by deregulation.

273. The industry as a whole remains composed essentially of small or medium-sized enterprises, frequently one-man businesses. There are therefore no natural monopoly features in this industry. There is however some evidence of concentration in the freight-forwarding segment (Australia) as deregulation has permitted the achievement of some economies of scale through grouping of shipments and the creation of hub-and-spoke structures for long-distance road haulage.

274. Wages in the industry have had an interesting evolution in some countries following deregulation. In the United States, trucking wages were substantially above the average level of manufacturing wages before deregulation, but dropped to rough parity with manufacturing wages following deregulation. A likely explanation for this, given the long-time strength of organised labour in US road transport, is that regulation created economic rents for hauliers which were shared in part with labour. Following the elimination of these rents with deregulation, wages fell correspondingly. Wages in the UK, however, do not seem to have fallen with deregulation; drivers' wages have recently been rising there.

275. Employment appears generally to have increased following deregulation. In France, for example, 20 000 new jobs have been created in the road freight sector within three years. New Zealand has likewise seen a substantial increase in employment in this sector.

276. There is no evidence of a worsening of safety performance of the road freight sector following deregulation. Indeed, in the United States according to recent accident data there has been an actual decline in accident rates during the 1980s. A similar result is seen in the UK, where the accident rate for heavy trucks decreased by more than half since deregulation in 1968, an improvement substantially greater than that achieved by private cars.

277. An interesting corollary to the accident statistics is the information that vehicle condition in the UK improved following deregulation, as measured by failure rates during safety inspections. This may be due to increased economic incentives under deregulation to use vehicles productively. Hauliers

thus may be improving maintenance practices to avoid unnecessary and costly time-wasting from failed safety inspections or breakdowns on the road.

b) Passenger road transport

278.   The idea that public transport services should be operated in the interests of providing adequate access to transport facilities by young, old and geographically isolated passengers remains a powerful motive for the continued operation of such services on uneconomic grounds, particularly in Europe.   Thus, in the past, local bus services have tended to be under public ownership and have been operated by municipal authorities with substantial subsidies.   Likewise, long-distance passenger transport has been heavily regulated as to routes, fares and entry.

279.   Given the social concerns behind passenger transport regulation, the experience of countries which have deregulated this sector is particularly important.   That experience is necessarily more limited because regulatory reform of passenger road transport has started much later than reform of freight transport and has been confined to relatively few countries so far. Nonetheless, it seems clear that deregulated passenger road transport can produce increased levels of service, decreased fares and innovations in the types of vehicles and services offered.

280.   The example of UK deregulation is particularly relevant.   In the United Kingdom, deregulation of long-distance services brought an immediate expansion in the number of services and a significant initial reduction in the level of fares on major routes.   However, those price cuts did not survive the collapse of the new consortium which had challenged the dominant national carrier.   The lack of new entry in spite of higher prices in the post-consortium period suggests that there are entry barriers due to the dominant incumbent carrier's extensive network of services and ownership of major coach terminals.

281.   Commuter services to London increased considerably immediately after deregulation but this development would seem to be limited by traffic congestion in London as well as railway and Underground competition.

282.   Another effect of privatisation and deregulation in the UK was a reduction in the level of subsidies which were awarded for unprofitable local services due to a change in the procedure for awarding them by putting them out to competitive tender.   A similar effect was observed in Sweden when the local authorities changed over to a competitive tendering system.

283.   Deregulation also produced the innovation of minibuses in the UK where demand was not sufficient to warrant the operation of conventional buses.   In the United States a similar development was noted in rural areas following deregulation where smaller vehicules have been used to feed passengers into the main terminals.

284.   Deregulation in the United States also produced a reduction in unprofitable scheduled services by Greyhound and Trailways.   Charter and special buses increased their activity following deregulation with many new entrants, enabling charter buses to increase their share of the market, accelerating a trend which was apparent already before deregulation.

Nonetheless, some small communities did lose service following US deregulation, suggesting a limited role for subsidies if social concerns require that transport services be provided.

285. All this does not mean that the industry, whether passenger or freight, is working under conditions of perfect competition or contestability. In particular, access to hub or terminal facilities and services are potentially troublesome in both sectors. The following chapter points to the need for vigilance by competition authorities to ensure that anti-competitive practices by private operators do not supplant the officially sanctioned restrictions formerly applied under regulation.

CHAPTER 4

HOW COMPETITION LAWS AND POLICIES APPLY TO ROAD TRANSPORT

OVERVIEW

286. Competition laws and policies have only recently been applied to road freight and passenger transport in most OECD countries. The existence of regulatory schemes in the road transport sector has, until relatively recently, inhibited the application of competition laws and policies. The extent of this limitation varies from country to country. Sometimes an exemption for road transport is specifically laid down in the main competition law. Other countries' laws merely state that the law does not apply to behaviour authorised under other regulations without specifying any particular sector or behaviour. The scope of the exemption is thus left to the competition authorities and courts to determine.

287. The one country where the sector remains totally excluded is Portugal but a draft bill is under discussion which would remedy that state of affairs.

288. In the European Communities, Council Regulation No. 1017/68 of 19th July 1968 specifically applies the EEC rules of competition to transport by rail, road and inland waterway.

289. Germany provides an example of specific exemption. The former Section 99(1) of the Act against Restraints of Competition stated that the Act did not apply to "... agreements .... of enterprises engaged in the transport or in the arrangement of transport of goods and persons, or to decisions and recommendations of associations of such enterprises pertaining to transportation services and connected services, if and insofar as the tariffs or conditions based on those agreements, decisions or recommendations are established or approved by or pursuant to an act or ordinance". The fifth Amendment to the Act abolishes this provision because it is basically declaratory. Similarly, Section 99(2) No. 1 a) of the Act provided for the exemption of road passenger transport networks and associations which are necessary for co-ordinating passenger transport services. Such networks and associations had however to be registered with the cartel authorities. The amendment to the Act retains this exemption but abolishes the registration requirement.

290. With the exception of Portugal, competition laws can often be applied to behaviour which has not been expressly approved by the regulatory authorities. In many countries there have been cases defining the respective limits of regulatory and competition law jurisdiction over conduct. In addition, the fact of public ownership of road transport undertakings may also exempt such undertakings from control under competition laws, as is the case in Belgium and Denmark.

291.   A 1976 French case defined the scope of a 1949 regulation which laid down a compulsory rate system to be observed by motor carriers. The Technical Commission on Cartels and Dominant Positions decided in this case that the rules of competition applied to all road freight activities. The professional bodies in the sector had used a common price list to fix minimum rates for services and they abandoned this list following the adverse opinion of the Commission.

292.   As deregulation has proceeded one can observe an increased reliance on the general provisions of competition law to deal with restrictive agreements, practices by individual firms, mergers and acquisitions. Thus, in the United Kingdom, since 1986 when bus services were deregulated, the legislation applies fully to all segments of the road transport industry. Australia, Canada, France, Germany, Ireland, Sweden and the United States have also applied their competition laws to the sector, though there remain some regulated activities which have been granted immunity or authorisation.

293.   Many of the enforcement actions have in fact been concerned with how far existing regulation does allow otherwise anti-competitive behaviour to take place. A good illustration of this is in Canada where a "regulated conduct defence" has developed to justify behaviour which has been approved by a regulatory authority. However this defence has been narrowed down and challenged when it has been shown that the regulator has not exercised his authority or where he has not been able to do so, for example, by not receiving adequate information from the firms involved or when the regulatory provisions also make the behaviour subject to the competition legislation (concurrent jurisdiction). Similarly, in the United States, collective rate-making at the state level may be immune under the state action doctrine, this doctrine having been held to apply only to states which have specifically approved collective rate-making among carriers and where the state actively reviewed the rates collectively agreed.

294.   There are only six countries where there has been extensive enforcement of the legislation against practices in the road transport sector -- Australia, Canada, France, Sweden, the United Kingdom and the United States. In the majority of Member countries even where some possibility exists under the competition legislation, there has been little or no enforcement in the road transport sector.

295.   Most of the actions that have been undertaken have been concerned with price or rate-fixing arrangements between carriers or with practices by dominant firms such as predatory pricing or behaviour designed to deny newcomers entry to the industry. There have been relatively few cases of enforcement of merger control legislation in OECD countries, unsurprising given the fragmented and unconcentrated nature of most of the segments of the road transport industry. There have, however, been some merger and acquisition cases in the inter-city buses and coaches sector in Germany, the United Kingdom and the United States and in the road freight transport sector in Sweden. There have also been several cases of collusive tendering or bid-rigging in tenders made by local authorities for school and other local bus services in several countries.

296.   Another method which has been used in several countries to promote competition in the still-regulated parts of the industry, where action under

competition laws is not possible, is for competition authorities to be empowered to submit briefs or memoranda in proceedings before regulatory boards or tribunals with the aim of advocating the most competitive solution to a regulatory issue which has arisen. Canada, Sweden, Switzerland and the United States are the countries where the competition authorities have been particularly active in this regard.

HORIZONTAL ARRANGEMENTS

297. Arrangements between road transport operators to fix rates, commissions or other trading conditions other than those approved under a regulatory scheme, have been generally found anti-competitive under most countries competition laws. For example, in Australia, an application by lorry owner drivers for authorisation of a negotiation and arbitration procedure for arriving at charges for carrying pre-mixed concrete in the Australian Capital Territory was denied by the Trade Practices Commission in 1988 because the arrangement involved a degree of inhibition of entry into the industry as well as an agreement on rate-setting, constituting a detriment to competition (71). The case is under appeal to the Trade Practices Tribunal.

298. In Canada, two cases of conspiracy involving for-hire general freight trucking and transport of household goods have been resolved in recent years. On 5th November 1979, an information was laid under section 32 of the Combines Investigation Act against 20 trucking companies and eleven individuals for allegedly conspiring to lessen competition unduly in the Western Canadian market for LTL transport services. In March 1988, a prohibition order under subsection 30(2) of the Act was obtained on consent. The order restrains the parties from doing acts or things constituting or directed toward the offence of conspiracy under section 32 with respect to the provision of inter-provincial transport of general merchandise, weighing 10 000 pounds or less, between Alberta and the other Western provinces. Notably, the order prohibits the practice of fixing or co-ordinating single line rates in the market -- i.e. collective rate-making.

299. The household goods case entailed an alleged conspiracy to prevent or lessen competition in inter-provincial transport of used (owned by shippers) household goods. Five Canadian van lines and their industry association or tariff bureau were involved. On 14th December 1983, the five van lines and their Tariff Bureau pleaded guilty to conspiring to lessen competition unduly in the inter-provincial transport of used household goods within Canada over a 17-year period starting in 1963. It was the Director's case that the conspiracy lessened competition unduly with respect to prices charged and the quality and quantity of services provided to the public. The five companies were fined a total of $250 000 and were made subject to a Prohibition Order. The order disbanded the tariff bureau and prohibited the five van lines and the moving companies affiliated with them from engaging in various forms of anti-competitive behaviour in the future.

300. In Denmark, since 1st January 1989 the road transport sector has come within the scope of the general competition rules (i.e. the Monopolies and Restrictive Practices Supervision Act 1955 and the Prices and Profits Act 1974).

301. The Monopolies Control Authority has carried out an investigation into the competitive effects of this liberalization in order to find out if notification and registration of the relevant trade organisations and their collegiate rules should be contemplated and/or other measures should be taken. The investigation showed that concurrently with the introduction of the new rules on deregulation, the Danish Haulage Contractors' Organisation decided to implement their own rules with the purpose of regulating the market in exactly the same way as it was regulated by the previous Act (access, routes and fares).

302. The Monopolies Control Authority has demanded notification of the Danish Haulage Contractors' Organisation in pursuance of Section 6(1) of the Monopolies and Restrictive Practices Supervision Act and has begun an investigation in pursuance of Section 11 into the body of rules and the practices of the organisation.

303. In France, in June 1988, the Competition Council condemned concerted practices between the French National Federation of Freight Forwarders and the main transport firms in the sector which were designed to effect uniform rate increases on 1st January and 1st July 1985 (72). Heavy fines were imposed on the parties by the Commission: 1 million francs on the National Federation of Freight Forwarders; 3 million francs on the firm CALBERSON and on the French Railways (SNCF) on account of its SERNAM service and 2 million francs on the firms DANZAS and MORY-TNTE. The Council's decision was upheld on appeal (73).

304. An earlier opinion of the Competition Commission concerned passenger transport in the Besançon area (74). The Commission considered that an economic interest group (GIE) composed of three passenger transport firms in the Besançon area was essentially designed to prevent new firms entering the local market and was therefore held to constitute a prohibited cartel agreement.

305. In Sweden, the two largest Swedish freight forwarding firms operated similar price lists based on uniform costs and changed their prices at the same time at the same percentage rates. The Competition Ombudsman considered that these practices were tantamount to price collaboration, if not collusive tendering. When one of the firms changed its pricing system and the date of putting price increases into effect, the Ombudsman decided to refrain from further action. Subsequently, however, the two firms plus other freight forwarders again began to co-operate as regards costing and this co-operation is currently under investigation.

306. In the United Kingdom, the Restrictive Trade Practices (Services) Order 1976 extended the scope of the legislation to include agreements relating to services. However the bus industry was exempted from the legislation until 1985 when the Transport Act ended the exemption. Since deregulation of the bus industry around 260 agreements have been submitted to the Office for examination, of which 142 were subject to registration. One hundred and fifteen of the agreements contained restrictions on fares and timetables having a significant effect on competition. The Director General advised the bus companies that unless these unacceptable restrictions were abandoned, he would refer the agreements to the Restrictive Practices Court. Most agreements have been acceptably amended. Two covert price fixing agreements were uncovered subsequently and these are to be referred to the Court.

307.   As   regards freight transport, the agreement of the British Association
of Removers (BAR) was registered with the Office of Fair Trading in October
1976.   Under the terms of its agreement, the association's members accepted
restrictions relating to inland removals and warehousing, on the charges to be
made for their services, conditions of contract and limitations on their
liability to customers, and an insurance scheme for overseas removals.   The
Office took the view that certain of the restrictions were significantly
anti-competitive.   Negotiations took place between the Office and BAR over a
number of years but no agreement was reached, and in 1985, the association
discontinued its recommendation to members that were the subject of the
negotiations.

308.   An agreement of the Road Haulage Association (RHA) consisting of its
code of practice, conditions of carriage and various conditions of
sub-contracting was registered in March 1977.   The agreement contained
restrictions on charges to be made by members and the terms and conditions on
which members provided their services. As in the case of the removals and
warehousing agreement, the Office found these restrictions to be
anti-competitive and, as a result of negotiations with the association, the RHA
withdrew its recommendation to members on charges at the end of 1977.

309.   In the United States, as mentioned in Chapter 2, the Motor Carrier Act
of 1980 changed the scope of antitrust immunity accorded to motor carrier rate
bureau activities.   Since 1st January 1984, carriers no longer have had
antitrust immunity for the collective discussion and setting of specific
single-line rates. Subject to certain procedural safeguards, however, immunity
continues for collective discussion and setting of general rate increases or
decreases after that date, provided that discussions are limited to industry
average costs rather than to individual markets or particular single-line
rates.   Immunity also remains for commodity classification changes, tariff
structure changes, and several non-price rate bureau activities.

310.   In 1984, in United States v. Niagara Frontier Tariff Bureau Inc. (75),
the United States obtained a consent decree against a motor carrier rate bureau
and its members that enjoined the defendants from fixing certain rates for a
period of ten years. The provisions of the decree restrict the defendants from
communicating with each other about planned independent rate announcements,
prohibit trucker agreements that restrain independent action and competition
for other carriers' customers, limit the scope of rate committee actions that
affect rates, and establish other restrictions on conduct by the defendants
that would have the effect of reducing competition among members.

311.   Two recent United States Federal Trade Commission cases in the freight
transport area have addressed the issue of whether particular conduct was
protected from antitrust action under the "state action" doctrine.   In 1987, an
administrative law judge ruled that although the Motor Transport Association of
Connecticut, Inc. ("MTAC") had set prices for the truck transport of goods in
the state, such action was protected from antitrust attack by the "state
action" doctrine. The association, a transport rating bureau, representing
approximately 585 competing motor carriers, had filed collective trucking rates
for various commodities with the state regulatory agency.   The judge, relying
on statutory delegation, the exercise of regulatory oversight, and active
supervision of the rates by a state board, concluded that the state intended
the programme to be exempt from the antitrust laws.   The judge therefore
dismissed the Commission's complaint (76).

312. The Commission recently decided another matter involving a transport rate bureau following an administrative law judge's ruling that the New England Motor Rate Bureau, Inc. (NEMRB) illegally conspired with its members to set rates and restrain competition in intra-state transportation of goods in Massachusetts and New Hampshire.

313. The principal issue in the case was whether the price-fixing conduct of the rate bureau was exempt from the antitrust laws under the "state action" doctrine. The judge found that New Hampshire did not have a clearly articulated state policy to replace competition in rate setting, and that neither New Hampshire nor Massachusetts actively supervised the intra-state rate-setting process. He did find, however, that the collective rate-setting done by the rate bureau in Rhode Island was exempt because of the extent and nature of that state's regulation (77).

314. The Commission on appeal ruled on 18th August 1989 (78) that the NEMRB activities in Massachusetts satisfied the first part of the test of the state action doctrine, that the State statute sanctioned collective rate-making among motor carriers, but did not satisfy the second part of the test in that state authority did not review the substance of merits of the tariff filings. The collective rate-making activity was therefore subject to antitrust scrutiny. The NEMRB's activities in New Hampshire were held not to satisfy either test since the New Hampshire authority had no power to control rates. The Commission's order requires the NEMRB to cancel all tariffs and terminate all agreements with states in which its rate bureau activities were not covered by the state action doctrine. Further, unless protected by state action, the NEMRB is prohibited from fixing carrier rates, filing collective rates, encouraging carriers to file specific rates, providing a forum for discussion of rates or passing non-public rate information between carriers (79).

315. In December 1989, the Antitrust Division petitioned the Inter-state Commerce Commission to issue an order requiring the Rocky Mountain Motor Tariff Bureau ("RMMTB") to show cause why the ICC should not revoke the antitrust immunity that permits the trucking companies composing RMMTB to collectively set periodic across-the-board rate increases, known as GRIs, for most transcontinental truck shipments and for shipments among various West Coast and Rocky Mountain states.

316. In 1987, the largest carriers in RMMTB began engaging in a practice that the Division contends gives the ICC grounds to revoke RMMTB's antitrust immunity. The practice began in April 1987, after the ICC suspended a 2.9 per cent GRI that had been set collectively by the members of RMMTB. Ordinarily, the Commission's suspension would have meant that the increase could not have gone into effect until the ICC reviewed the increase and determined it to be reasonable. However, within three days after the Commission issued its suspension order, the principal carriers in RMMTB began filing identical 2.9 per cent increases as "independent actions," a type of rate filing that is to within the scope of the RMMTB's antitrust immunity. Under normal ICC procedures, the RMMTB carriers' allegedly "independent" rate increases promptly went into effect without being reviewed for reasonableness. Since then, the same scenario has been repeated four more times. The ICC has not yet acted on the Division's petition.

COLLUSIVE TENDERING

317.   Cases of collusive tendering have occurred in some countries, mostly in
connection with the provision of local bus services or for special forms of
transport such as school buses.

318.   Thus in Canada, three companies and one individual were convicted in
1981 for bid-rigging in a municipality in Ontario in the supply of bus
services.   The French Commission on Cartels and Dominant Positions condemned
practices by several Departmental Associations of Carriers as well as the
National Road Transport Federation which were designed to allocate markets, fix
tendering prices and impose price increases (80).   In Sweden, local hauliers
were found guilty of violating the ban on collusive tendering by colluding in
the submission of tenders to a local authority.

ABUSE OF MARKET POWER

319.   Predatory pricing has been a practice which has been the subject of
attention on the part of competition authorities in Australia and the United
Kingdom.   In addition, the issue of access to bus stations has come up in the
United Kingdom.

320.   In Australia, in 1986 a road freight enterprise, the successful tenderer
for a State Government grain carriage contract between inland storage
facilities and sea ports, commenced a private action against the State
Railways.   The enterprise sought an interim injunction against the Railway
which, having been an unsuccessful tenderer for the contract, had reacted by
offering farmers a paddock-to-port service effectively undercutting the
enterprise's prices.   It was argued that the Railway was offering prices which
did not reflect fair competitive activity because the farm-to-rail sector would
have to operate at a loss and, hence, the activity was predatory.   The
enterprise argued that the Railway had substantial market power in those areas
of the State of Western Australia where it had an effective statutory monopoly
for grain carriage.

321.   The Court found that the enterprise had raised a serious question to be
tried but declined on the balance of convenience to grant an interim injunction
given that there would have then been substantial disruption to arrangements
negotiated between the Railway and farmers and that any losses could be
rectified by a later award of damages if the enterprise were to succeed at a
full hearing (81).

322.   In the United Kingdom, there have been several interventions by the
Office of Fair Trading in the local bus industry on account of allegations of
predatory pricing or other forms of exclusionary behaviour by dominant local
bus companies.

323.   The first formal investigation under the Competition Act was launched on
19th June 1987.   It followed a complaint by a small bus operator on the Isle of
Wight that Southern Vectis Omnibus Company Ltd (SV), a privatised ex-National
Bus Company subsidiary and the major local bus service operator on the island,
had refused to grant access to its bus station at Newport.   The operator
claimed that this restricted his ability to pick up and set down passengers,

thus putting him at a competitive disadvantage and restricting passengers' choice of service.

324.   Under section 82 of the Transport Act 1985 bus stations owned by local authorities and passenger transport executives must provide access to all bus service operators on a non-discriminatory basis, but such a requirement does not exist for privately owned bus stations. The competition legislation was however amended so that the Director General could investigate cases where it appeared that denial of access to other bus service operators could be anti-competitive.

325.   As a result of the investigation it was decided that SV's policy of denying other operators use of the bus station restricted competition in that both existing and prospective competitors were prevented from using an essential means of bringing their bus services to passengers' attention. The investigation was concluded when SV gave undertakings to allow other bus operators to use its bus station at Newport, Isle of Wight.

326.   Three   further formal investigations have been carried out under section 3 of the Competition Act. Each concerned allegations that, since deregulation, the companies have excluded, or sought to exclude, new operators from the market by predatory behaviour, i.e. predatory pricing, route swamping (overbusing).   In order to assess whether a firm's behaviour is predatory the Office considers three factors:

- whether the structure and characteristics of the particular market are such as to make predation feasible. Feasibility involves the consideration of entry barriers, competition from other forms of transport, the ability to finance losses and to establish a reputation for toughness in reacting to new entrants;

- the relationship between revenue and costs. The Office regards as predatory a failure to cover variable and semi-variable costs, but the extent to which a failure to also cover allocated overheads is predatory is assessed on a case-by-case basis. The Office has regarded the covering of the relevant share of overhead costs (garage, engineering and administration) as important when considering a network or sub-network of routes;

- evidence on the motives and intention of the firm, including relevant evidence from its behaviour in other local markets.

327.   Two of these investigations were launched on 22nd June 1988. The first resulted from a complaint by a small bus operator that South Yorkshire Transport Ltd had reintroduced services on the route between Sheffield and High Green, from which it had previously withdrawn, and had been charging uneconomically low fares. The investigation found that South Yorks had engaged in predatory behaviour. The second investigation followed a complaint from another small bus operator that West Yorkshire Road Car Company Ltd (WYRC) was charging uneconomically low fares on the route between Crosshills and Skipton. The investigation concluded that, while WYRC was responding to the entry of competition, it was not engaging in an anti-competitive practice. A third investigation launched on 22nd March 1989, found that Highland Scottish Omnibuses Limited, a long-established operator and part of the publicly owned

Scottish Bus Group, had by a combination of its fare levels and raising capacity by 60 per cent acted predatorily in an attempt to eliminate competition.

328. A fourth investigation under section 3 of the Competition Act was launched on 13th June 1989. It concluded, given the profitability of the services in question, that Hull City Transport were not engaging in an anti-competitive practice.

329. Formal investigations, such as those described above, arise from complaints made to the Office. Each complaint is subjected to a preliminary investigation and may be resolved without recourse to a formal investigation. As of 31st January 1990, some 202 complaints had been received since deregulation in 1986. The most common causes for complaints have been predatory behaviour (42 per cent of cases) and the operation of the subsidised sector (24 per cent of cases).

330. It may be that complaints received by the Office are symptomatic of the behavioural changes that are taking place in the local bus industry as a result of deregulation. Inter-company relationships -- such as route-sharing -- established over a long period in a heavily regulated environment will take some time to move to a competitive basis. The nature of competition in local bus services will be established by companies "testing" their competitive strategies while the Office attempts to prevent market failure. At present, it appears that competition has taken place principally between large operators and new entrants. Competition between large operators still appears to be limited. Small scale entry often takes place initially on the subsidised routes following a successful bid in competitive tendering. Problems have arisen when established operators have registered a commercial service on the route following failure in the tendering process. In practice this has led to the withdrawal of the subsidy and often exit of the new entrant.

MERGERS AND ACQUISITIONS

331. There has been some enforcement of merger control provisions in four countries -- Germany, Sweden, the United Kingdom and the United States. Most of the cases have involved small companies and the mergers have not been found to be anti-competitive. It should be noted that in two countries -- Canada and the United States -- there is concurrent jurisdiction over mergers with the relevant regulatory agency, the National Transportation Agency and the Interstate Commerce Commission respectively.

332. In Germany, most mergers in the road freight transport sector have been in response to technological change as well as to the demands of the single European market and have involved firms with relatively small market shares. Thus no merger in the sector has been prohibited by the Federal Cartel Office. For example, in 1986 an acquisition by Rhenus, AG, the Veba Group's freight forwarding and transport company, of Weichelt was allowed to proceed -- the participating companies commanding less than 5 per cent of the package freight market. An acquisition in 1988 by Franz Haniel and Cie. Gmbh, of an important regional freight forwarder was considered not to create a position of market domination in the package freight sector nor did it amount to the strengthening of such a position. A partial acquisition by Salvesen PLC of the food trade

and frozen distribution interests of Unilever Langnese-Iglo in 1987 raised no objections as the market shares were small and there were a large number of competitors. The Bundeskartellamt was not able to review the sale of a 22.5 per cent holding in the transport company Schenker by the Deutsche Bundesbahn to VEBA AG because the stake was below the 25 per cent threshhold required for action by the Office.

333.   In <u>Sweden</u>, the Competition Ombudsman has intervened against an acquisition by the largest freight forwarding firm which would have given it a strengthened position both in international and domestic forwarding. The intervention resulted in the divestment of parts of the acquired enterprise to reduce the dominance.

334.   In the <u>United Kingdom</u>, since the privatisation and splitting up of the National Bus Company, the Office of Fair Trading has considered eleven mergers in the bus industry. One of these -- the acquisition by Badgerline Holdings Ltd of Midland Red West Holdings Ltd -- was referred to the Monopolies and Mergers Commission in October 1988, the Secretary of State considering that the merger raised questions of competition in the Bristol and Avon area especially with regard to Local Authority contract bus services. The Commission's report, published in March 1989, concluded that the merger might be expected to operate against the public interest. Two areas of particular concern were:

- the practice whereby Badgerline, having de-registered certain commercial services, re-registered them after failing to win the contracts for the subsidised services which replaced them; and

- the loss of Cityline as a major competitor for the Avon County Council's contract services.

The Secretary of State has accepted undertakings from Badgerline Holdings Limited in relation to its operation of contract bus services in the Bristol and Avon area. These undertakings have been offered as a result of discussions between Badgerline and the Director General of Fair Trading following the publication of the Monopolies and Mergers Commission's report.

335.   In the <u>United States</u>, the Antitrust Division participated in proceedings before the Interstate Commerce Commission ("ICC") concerning the proposed acquisition by the country's largest nationwide bus system, Greyhound Lines, Inc., of its sole remaining nationwide competitor, Continental Trailways Lines, Inc. The Division initially urged the ICC not to approve the merger until Greyhound proved its contention that Trailways qualified as a "failing company" under the Division's merger guidelines and relevant judicial decisions. After a thorough inquiry into Trailways' financial situation, the Division concluded that the transaction met the requirements of the failing company doctrine and withdrew its objection to the transaction. On May 17th 1988 the ICC approved the merger.

336.   In November 1989, the Division filed a Complaint at the ICC against summary approval of the proposed merger of Brink's Incorporated and Loomis Armored, Inc. Brink's and Loomis are the first and second largest companies engaged in the provision of the protective transportation and related services for valuable commodities by armoured car and air courier service. The Division has been granted discovery by the ICC, and continues to investigate the transaction.

NOTES AND REFERENCES

1. See Report by OECD Scientific Experts Group (1986) "Technico-Economic Analysis of the Role of Road Freight Transport", p. 6.

2. Statistical Trends in Transport 1965-1986, ECMT, 1989, p. 42 (ECMT Report).

3. OECD Scientific Experts Group (1986), op. cit., p. 50.

4. Austria, Belgium, Denmark, Finland, France, Germany, Italy, Luxembourg, Netherlands, Norway, Spain, Sweden, Switzerland, Turkey and the United Kingdom.

5. OECD Scientific Experts Group (1986), op. cit., p. 65.

6. See Australian National Road Freight Industry Inquiry, Report, September 1984, pp. 48-53.

7. Canadian reply to questionnaire, p. 17, Table 16.

8. Statement of Reese H. Taylor Jr. Chairman, Interstate Commerce Commission before the Surface Transportation Subcommittee of the House Committee on Public Ways and Transportation on Implementation of the Motor Carrier Act of 1980, November 7th 1985, pp. 12-13.

9. ECMT report, Table G(c), p. 29.

10. Report of the committee of enquiry into the road haulage industry (the Geddes report), HMSO, London, 1965.

11. Council on Wage and Price Stability, "The Value of Motor Carrier Operating Rights", p. 7, (June 9th 1977).

12. T. Moore, "The Beneficiaries of Trucking Regulation", 21 Journal of Law and Economics, 1978, p. 327, 342.

13. W. Blumenthal "Anticompetitive Threats in Motor Coverage under Alternative Regulatory Schemes", Harvard Law School paper 1979 p. 105.

14. N. Jones, Jr. "On Removing Operating and Empty Backhaul Restrictions" in P. MacAvoy and J. Snow, Regulation of Entry and Pricing in Truck Transportation, pp. 25-26 (Washington D.C., 1977).

15. W. Allen, S. Lonergan and D. Plane, "Examination of the Unregulated Trucking Experiences in New Jersey", DOT Mimeo (1978).

16. S. Breyer, "Regulation and its Reform", Harvard University Press, 1982, p. 230.

17. See Acts of the Council of Ministers of the ECMT (1953-1982), ECMT, Paris, 1983.

18. National Road Freight Industry Inquiry, op. cit., p. 13-14.

19. Ibid.

20. Hughes and Vale Pty Ltd v. New South Wales (No. 1) (1954) 93 CLR 1 and Hughes and Vale (No. 2) (1955) 93 CLR 127.

21. See Intrastate Bus Services in New South Wales, Trial Entry Liberalisation, Occasional Paper 85, Federal Bureau of Transport Economics, Australian Government Publishing Service, Canberra, 1987.

22. This summary is based on Maurice Girault: La déréglementation des transports routiers de marchandises en France, Observatoire Economique et Statistique des Transports, mars 1989, pp. 37-8.

23. Id. p. 40.

24. Id. p. 50.

25. Id. p. 42.

26. Bjørn Gildestad: The Norwegian Approach to Road Freight Deregulation Policy, paper presented to Seminar on Road Transport Deregulation organised by OECD Road Research Unit and INRETS, Paris, 2-4 November 1988 (Hereinafter OECD/INRETS Seminar) p. 8.

27. This account of Swedish deregulation is based on an English summary of a study by Lars Kritz: Transport Policy and the Lorries -- a Study of the Effects of Regulation and Deregulation (Swedish title: Transportpolitiken och lastbilarna -- En studie av regleringar och deras effecter), Almqvist and Wiksell International, Stockholm, 1976.

28. Lars Kritz, Transport Policy and Transport Developments in Sweden, Federation of Swedish Industries, August 1981.

29. J. Palmer: Deregulation in Great Britain: Road Haulage, Express Coaches and the Railways. Paper presented at OECD and INRETS Seminar, op. cit. footnote 32.

30. Ibid.

31. Road Haulage Operators Licensing: Report of the Independent Committee of Inquiry, HMSO 1978.

32. J. Palmer, op. cit., see note 35.

33. Report of the Inquiry into Lorries, People and the Environment, to the Minister of Transport, HMSO 1980.

34.   J. Palmer, op. cit.

35.   Bleasdale, C. (1983) Coaches: a case of wasteful competition, Modern Railways, Vol. 42, No. 438.

36.   J. Palmer, op. cit., see note 35.

37.   Russell P. Kilvington, The Impact of Deregulation of Express Coach Services in Great Britain, paper presented to OECD/INRETS Seminar on Road Transport Deregulation, op. cit., pp. 2-3.

38.   Peter R. White: Deregulation of Bus and Coach Services in Britain from 1980. Paper presented to OECD/INRETS Seminar, op. cit., p. 3.

39.   Ibid.

40.   Ibid., p. 9.

41.   "Buses", Government White Paper on Bus Policy, Department of Transport, Scottish Office, Welsh Office (HMSO) 1984.

42.   The account which follows is based essentially on a paper by B.S. Clough, "Monitoring Bus Deregulation - TRRL's National Programme", presented at the OECD/INRETS Seminar, see footnote 32.

43.   Ibid.

44.   Bus Deregulation in Great Britain: a review of the first year by R.J. Balcombe, J.M. Hopkin and K.E. Perrett, Department of Transport TRRL Research Report 161, 1988, pp. 20-21.

45.   Turner R.P. and White P.R. (1987). NBC's urban minibuses: a review and financial appraisal. Department of Transport report CR 42.

46.   Joseph Canny and Edward Rastatter: US Trucking Deregulation since 1980. Paper presented to OECD/INRETS Seminar, op. cit., p. 1.

47.   Morrison, S.A. and C. Winston: "Transportation Route Structures Under Deregulation: Assessments Activated by the Airline Experience", American Economic Review, Vol. 75, May 1985, No. 2, pp. 57-61.

48.   C.J. Pearce and Terence Brown: The Effects of Transport Deregulation on Transport Intermediaries, paper presented at OECD/INRETS Seminar, 1988, p. 2.

49.   Michael W. Pustary: Regulatory Reform of Motor Freight Carriage in the United States, Rivesta Internazionale di Economia dei Transporti, Vol. 10, 1983, p. 273.

50.   Veier F.J. and Stone, G.B.: Review of the Delaney-Evans debate, Report prepared for the United States Department of Transportation, Washington D.C., 1988.

51.   Statement of Reese H. Taylor, Jr., op. cit., p. 3.

52. Ibid., p. 16.

53. Ibid., p. 17-18.

54. Canny and Rastatter, op. cit., p. 3.

55. Ibid., p. 4.

56. Ibid., p. 5.

57. Ibid.

58. Ibid., p. 5.

59. Ibid., p. 5.

60. Paul P. Jovanis: Motor Carrier Safety and Economic Deregulation: US Experiences, European Prospects. Paper presented at OECD/INRETS Seminar, op. cit., pp. 5-7.

61. Ibid., p. 2 and Table 1, p. 6.

62. Interstate Commerce Commission 1987 Annual Report, April 1988.

63. Karen Borlary Phillips: Intercity Bus Deregulation: Origins and Effects. Paper presented to OECD/INRETS Seminar, 1988, p. 11.

64. Statement of Heather J. Gradison, Chairman, Interstate Commerce Commission, before the Subcommittee on Surface Transportation of the Senate Committee on Commerce, Science and Transportation on Passenger Bus Transportation, August 25, 1988.

65. Ibid.

66. Clint V. Oster and C. Kurt Zorn: The Impacts of Regulatory Reform on Intercity Bus Service (Washington DC, US DOT, University Research Office, 1984) p. 1.

67. Joseph Holt, The Impacts of Bus Deregulation in Illinois (Springfield, IL, Mimeo paper 1986) pp. 3-4.

68. Interstate Commerce Commission, Intercity Bus Industry, January 1984, p. 75.

69. Mary Kihl, The Impacts of Deregulation on Passenger Transportation in Small Towns, Transportation Quarterly, Vol. 42, No. 2, April 1988, p. 259.

70. Helen Tauchen, Frederic D. Fravel and Norman Gilbert: Cost Structure of the Inter-City Bus Industry, Journal of Transport Economics and Policy, January 1983, p. 35.

71. Application No. A90486 determined on 12th October 1988.

72.   Decision of 21st June 1988 of the Competition Council relating to practices in the freight forwarding sector.

73.   Judgment of the Paris Court of Appeal of 21st December 1988.

74.   Competition Commission opinion of 22nd February 1979 in the case Triponney v. Transgroup.

75.   1982-2 Trade Cases (CCH) paragraph 66, 167 (WDNY 1984).

76.   See Motor Transport Association of Connecticut, Inc., Docket No. 9186 (1983-1987 Transfer Binder) Trade Reg. Rep. (CCII), paragraph 22,424.

77.   See New England Motor Rate Bureau Inc., Docket No. 9170 (1983-1987 Transfer Binder) Trade Reg. Rep. paragraph 22,417

78.   57 Antitrust and Trade Regulation Reporter 242 (24th August 1989).

79.   Id.

80.   Opinion of 8th February 1974 of the Technical Commission on Cartels and Dominant Positions: Agreement between enterprises engaged in road transport.

81.   QD Transport Pty Ltd v. The Western Australian Government Railways Commission (1987) Australian Trade Practices Reports 40-761.

WHERE TO OBTAIN OECD PUBLICATIONS – OÙ OBTENIR LES PUBLICATIONS DE L'OCDE

Argentina – Argentine
Carlos Hirsch S.R.L.
Galería Güemes, Florida 165, 4° Piso
1333 Buenos Aires   Tel. 30.7122, 331.1787 y 331.2391
Telegram: Hirsch–Baires
Telex: 21112 UAPE–AR. Ref. s/2901
Telefax:(1)331–1787

Australia – Australie
D.A. Book (Aust.) Pty. Ltd.
648 Whitehorse Road, P.O.B 163
Mitcham, Victoria 3132   Tel. (03)873.4411
Telex: AA37911 DA BOOK
Telefax: (03)873.5679

Austria – Autriche
OECD Publications and Information Centre
4 Simrockstrasse
5300 Bonn (Germany)   Tel. (0228)21.60.45
Telex: 8 86300 Bonn
Telefax: (0228)26.11.04

Gerold & Co.
Graben 31
Wien I   Tel. (0222)533.50.14

Belgium – Belgique
Jean De Lannoy
Avenue du Roi 202
B–1060 Bruxelles   Tel. (02)538.51.69/538.08.41
Telex: 63220   Telefax: (02) 538.08.41

Canada
Renouf Publishing Company Ltd.
1294 Algoma Road
Ottawa, ON K1B 3W8   Tel. (613)741.4333
Telex: 053–4783   Telefax: (613)741.5439
Stores:
61 Sparks Street
Ottawa, ON K1P 5R1   Tel. (613)238.8985
211 Yonge Street
Toronto, ON M5B 1M4   Tel. (416)363.3171

Federal Publications
165 University Avenue
Toronto, ON M5H 3B8   Tel. (416)581.1552
Telefax: (416)581.1743

Les Publications Fédérales
1185 rue de l'Université
Montréal, PQ H3B 3A7   Tel.(514)954–1633

Les Éditions La Liberté Inc.
3020 Chemin Sainte–Foy
Sainte–Foy, PQ G1X 3V6   Tel. (418)658.3763
Telefax: (418)658.3763

Denmark – Danemark
Munksgaard Export and Subscription Service
35, Norre Sogade, P.O. Box 2148
DK–1016 Kobenhavn K   Tel. (45 33)12.85.70
Telex: 19431 MUNKS DK   Telefax: (45 33)12.93.87

Finland – Finlande
Akateeminen Kirjakauppa
Keskuskatu 1, P.O. Box 128
00100 Helsinki   Tel. (358 0)12141
Telex: 125080   Telefax: (358 0)121.4441

France
OECD/OCDE
Mail Orders/Commandes par correspondance:
2 rue André–Pascal
75775 Paris Cedex 16   Tel. (1)45.24.82.00
Bookshop/Librairie:
33, rue Octave–Feuillet
75016 Paris   Tel. (1)45.24.81.67
   (1)45.24.81.81
Telex: 620 160 OCDE
Telefax: (33–1)45.24.85.00

Librairie de l'Université
12a, rue Nazareth
13602 Aix–en–Provence   Tel. 42.26.18.08

Germany – Allemagne
OECD Publications and Information Centre
Schedestrasse 7
5300 Bonn 1   Tel. (0228)21.60.45
Telefax: (0228)26.11.04

Greece – Grèce
Librairie Kauffmann
28 rue du Stade
105 64 Athens   Tel. 322.21.60
Telex: 218187 LIKA Gr

Hong Kong
Swindon Book Co. Ltd.
13 – 15 Lock Road
Kowloon, Hongkong   Tel. 366 80 31
Telex: 50 441 SWIN HX
Telefax: 739 49 75

Iceland – Islande
Mál Mog Menning
Laugavegi 18, Pósthólf 392
121 Reykjavik   Tel. 15199/24240

India – Inde
Oxford Book and Stationery Co.
Scindia House
New Delhi 110001   Tel. 331.5896/5308
Telex: 31 61990 AM IN
Telefax: (11)332.5993
17 Park Street
Calcutta 700016   Tel. 240832

Indonesia – Indonésie
Pdii–Lipi
P.O. Box 269/JKSMG/88
Jakarta 12790   Tel. 583467
Telex: 62 875

Ireland – Irlande
TDC Publishers – Library Suppliers
12 North Frederick Street
Dublin 1   Tel. 744835/749677
Telex: 33530 TDCP EI   Telefax : 748416

Italy – Italie
Libreria Commissionaria Sansoni
Via Benedetto Fortini, 120/10
Casella Post. 552
50125 Firenze   Tel. (055)645415
Telex: 570466   Telefax: (39.55)641257
Via Bartolini 29
20155 Milano   Tel. 365083
La diffusione delle pubblicazioni OCSE viene assicurata dalle
principali librerie ed anche da:
Editrice e Libreria Herder
Piazza Montecitorio 120
00186 Roma   Tel. 679.4628
Telex: NATEL I 621427
Libreria Hoepli
Via Hoepli 5
20121 Milano   Tel. 865446
Telex: 31.33.95   Telefax: (39.2)805.2886
Libreria Scientifica
Dott. Lucio de Biasio "Aeiou"
Via Meravigli 16
20123 Milano   Tel. 807679
Telefax: 800175

Japan– Japon
OECD Publications and Information Centre
Landic Akasaka Building
2–3–4 Akasaka, Minato–ku
Tokyo 107   Tel. 586.2016
Telefax: (81.3)584.7929

Korea – Corée
Kyobo Book Centre Co. Ltd.
P.O. Box 1658, Kwang Hwa Moon
Seoul   Tel. (REP)730.78.91
Telefax: 735.0030

Malaysia/Singapore – Malaisie/Singapour
University of Malaya Co–operative Bookshop Ltd.
P.O. Box 1127, Jalan Pantai Baru 59100
Kuala Lumpur
Malaysia   Tel. 756.5000/756.5425
Telefax: 757.3661
Information Publications Pte. Ltd.
Pei–Fu Industrial Building
24 New Industrial Road No. 02–06
Singapore 1953   Tel. 283.1786/283.1798
Telefax: 284.8875

Netherlands – Pays–Bas
SDU Uitgeverij
Christoffel Plantijnstraat 2
Postbus 20014
2500 EA's–Gravenhage   Tel. (070 3)78.99.11
Voor bestellingen: Tel. (070 3)78.98.80
Telex: 32486 stdru   Telefax: (070 3)47.63.51

New Zealand – Nouvelle–Zélande
Government Printing Office
Customer Services
33 The Esplanade – P.O. Box 38–900
Petone, Wellington
Tel. (04) 685–555   Telefax: (04)685–333

Norway – Norvège
Narvesen Info Center – NIC
Bertrand Narvesens vei 2
P.O. Box 6125 Etterstad
0602 Oslo 6   Tel. (02)57.33.00
Telex: 79668 NIC N   Telefax: (02)68.19.01

Pakistan
Mirza Book Agency
65 Shahrah Quaid–E–Azam
Lahore 3   Tel. 66839
Telex: 44886 UBL PK. Attn: MIRZA BK

Portugal
Livraria Portugal
Rua do Carmo 70–74
Apart. 2681
1117 Lisboa Codex   Tel. 347.49.82/3/4/5
Telefax: 37 02 64

Singapore/Malaysia – Singapour/Malaisie
See "Malaysia/Singapore – "Voir "Malaisie/Singapour"

Spain – Espagne
Mundi–Prensa Libros S.A.
Castelló 37, Apartado 1223
Madrid 28001   Tel. (91) 431.33.99
Telex: 49370 MPLI   Telefax: 575 39 98
Libreria Internacional AEDOS
Consejo de Ciento 391
08009 –Barcelona   Tel. (93) 301–86–15
Telefax: (93) 317–01–41

Sweden – Suède
Fritzes Fackboksföretaget
Box 16356, S 103 27 STH
Regeringsgatan 12
DS Stockholm   Tel. (08)23.89.00
Telex: 12387 Telefax: (08)20.50.21
Subscription Agency/Abonnements:
Wennergren–Williams AB
Box 30004
104 25 Stockholm   Tel. (08)54.12.00
Telex: 19937 Telefax: (08)50.82.86

Switzerland – Suisse
OECD Publications and Information Centre
Schedestrasse 7
5300 Bonn 1   Tel. (0228)21.60.45
Telefax: (0228)26.11.04
Librairie Payot
6 rue Grenus
1211 Genève 11   Tel. (022)731.89.50
Telex: 28356
Subscription Agency – Service des Abonnements
4 place Pépinet – BP 3312
1002 Lausanne   Tel. (021)341.33.31
Telefax: (021)341.33.45
Maditec S.A.
Ch. des Palettes 4
1020 Renens/Lausanne   Tel. (021)635.08.65
Telefax: (021)635.07.80
United Nations Bookshop/Librairie des Nations–Unies
Palais des Nations
1211 Genève 10   Tel. (022)734.60.11 (ext. 48.72)
Telex: 289696 (Attn: Sales)
Telefax: (022)733.98.79

Taiwan – Formose
Good Faith Worldwide Int'l. Co. Ltd.
9th Floor, No. 118, Sec. 2
Chung Hsiao E. Road
Taipei   Tel. 391.7396/391.7397
Telefax: (02) 394.9176

Thailand – Thaïlande
Suksit Siam Co. Ltd.
1715 Rama IV Road, Samyan
Bangkok 5   Tel. 251.1630

Turkey – Turquie
Kültur Yayinlari Is–Türk Ltd. Sti.
Atatürk Bulvari No. 191/Kat. 21
Kavaklidere/Ankara   Tel. 25.07.60
Dolmabahce Cad. No. 29
Besiktas/Istanbul   Tel. 160.71.88
Telex: 43482B

United Kingdom – Royaume–Uni
HMSO
Gen. enquiries   Tel. (071) 873 0011
Postal orders only:
P.O. Box 276, London SW8 5DT
Personal Callers HMSO Bookshop
49 High Holborn, London WC1V 6HB
Telex: 297138 Telefax: 071 873 8463
Branches at: Belfast, Birmingham, Bristol, Edinburgh,
Manchester

United States – États–Unis
OECD Publications and Information Centre
2001 L Street N.W., Suite 700
Washington, D.C. 20036–4095   Tel. (202)785.6323
Telefax: (202)785.0350

Venezuela
Libreria del Este
Avda F. Miranda 52, Aptdo. 60337
Edificio Galipán
Caracas 106   Tel. 951.1705/951.2307/951.1297
Telegram: Libreste Caracas

Yugoslavia – Yougoslavie
Jugoslovenska Knjiga
Knez Mihajlova 2, P.O. Box 36
Beograd   Tel. 621.992
Telex: 12466 jk bgd

Orders and inquiries from countries where Distributors have
not yet been appointed should be sent to: OECD Publications
Service, 2 rue André–Pascal, 75775 Paris Cedex 16, France.
Les commandes provenant de pays où l'OCDE n'a pas encore
désigné de distributeur devraient être adressées à : OCDE,
Service des Publications, 2, rue André–Pascal, 75775 Paris
Cedex 16, France.

10/90

OECD PUBLICATIONS, 2, rue André-Pascal, 75775 PARIS CEDEX 16
PRINTED IN FRANCE
(24 90 03 1) ISBN 92-64-13428-X - No. 45355 1990